A HOSER'S GUIDE TO CANADIAN HISTORY

A REALLY GOOD ATTEMPT TO EXPLAIN HOW WE GOT HERE

KIRT PURDY

Peasantry PRESS

Library and Archives Canada Cataloguing in Publication

Purdy, Kirt, 1970-, author
        A hoser's guide to Canadian history : a really good
attempt to explain how we got here / Kirt Purdy.

Issued in print and electronic formats.
ISBN 978-0-9940210-5-2 (paperback).--ISBN 978-0-9940210-6-9
(ebook)

        1. Canada--History--Humor. 2. Canadian wit and humor
(English). I. Title.

FC173.P87 2016   C818'.602   C2016-901016-3
                                           C2016-901017-1

Peasantry PRESS

PEASANTRY PRESS
Winnipeg, Manitoba, Canada
www.peasantrypress.com

*For my Mom, who constantly shared
her love of books with me.*

INTRODUCTION

Thank you for purchasing/borrowing/stealing this book. If you are reading about Canadian history, it means you aren't out destroying society by taking selfies with your phone, with which you've never made an actual phone call.

The problem with writing a history book is that references, which seemed fairly accurate during the production of the book, can become rather foolish-looking due to certain unforeseen events. These heartless happenings have positively no regard for the many hours I spent writing this thing. For instance, I take a few jabs at the Toronto Blue Jays, who have for 22 years exited the realm of relevance in baseball around mid-July. This year, they decided to win a few more games here and there and made it to the playoffs. I am concerned that hardcore Jays' fans will seek litigious action against my person for suggesting that the 22-year post-season drought would never end. (In contrast, I am not worried at all about the shots I took at the Toronto Maple Leafs, who will no doubt continue to prove that any player wearing a Leafs' jersey instantly forgets how to skate.)

It is also possible that the government of Canada, in its inexorable struggle to make everyone feel welcome (except its own citizens), will pass a law saying that anyone who speaks ill of Louis Riel will be hanged in both official languages. Schools will teach that Sir John A. Macdonald was simply a crazy, drunk Scotsman who became our first Prime Minister when he lost a poutine-eating contest. (The winner got to retire with a full pension and a cabin on Lake Muskoka.) But I digress.

Seriously, I do thank you for reading this book. You will learn many neato things about Canada and its storied past: some good, some bad, many perplexing. My hope is that you will be driven to discover even more of our shared history, and then head out, corner your friends, and spread the good word!

Cheers,

Kirt Purdy

Chief Historian and Semi-Pro Ballroom Dancer

CHAPTER ONE
IN THE BEGINNING

At the dawn of civilization, North America was empty. There were, of course, trees, rocks, animals, and talk show hosts, but no intelligent life.

Suddenly, people showed up. At time of writing, we still aren't absolutely sure about how, when, or where this happened, but there are three theories that have been offered by experts.

THEORY 1
"LAND BRIDGE"

THEORY 3
"FLIGHT DIVERTED"

THEORY 2
"ISLAND HOP
IN CANOES"

Theory #1 – People came from Siberia across the Beringia land bridge that has since disappeared due to rising ocean levels.

Theory #2 – People came from Polynesia to the coast of South America via canoes, then walked up to North America.

Theory #3 – People arrived on a flight that was diverted from Paris because of snow in Moscow. Their luggage was lost.

I'm partial to #3, but people smarter than me say it is probably a combination of #1 and #2. When I refer to #3 as a distinct possibility, and openly scoff at the chances of crossing the mighty Pacific Ocean in shallow canoes, those same people eventually smack me in the face with a lunch tray.

But, no matter. People got here somehow, some way, and we need to move on.

Most scholars agree that the First Nations People arrived here between 10,000 and 20,000 years ago. Unfortunately, they arrived on New Year's Day, and Tim Hortons was closed for renovations, so they had to find an alternate source of food. Food was abundant in North America – from fish to fowl, and berries to squirrels. Another form of food was the 2,000 pound buffalo. The buffalo herds were so large that they stretched from the Rocky Mountains to Winnipeg, which hadn't been invented yet. Since it took weeks for the people to walk around them, they started to get hungry. Then, one day, out of frustration, a hungry man (we'll call him 'Hank') whacked a buffalo (we'll call him 'Stan') on the head with a stick. This happened near what would become Calgary, and it

BUFFALO HERD

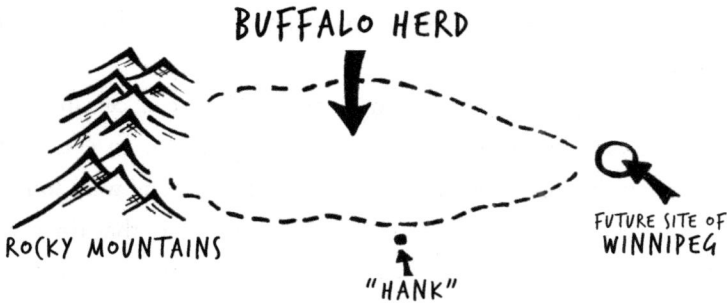

ROCKY MOUNTAINS

"HANK"

FUTURE SITE OF
WINNIPEG

started a stampede. This stampede is commemorated with the annual festival known as Boxing Day.

The herd of buffalo chased Hank for a while, until he got the bright idea to play dead. They never found Hank, but the buffalo were so blinded with rage at the assault on Stan that they jumped right off a cliff and smashed their heads in on the valley floor below. This site is now called, for obvious reasons, "Head-Smashed-In-Buffalo-Jump-Thanks-To-Hank-And-His-Stupid-Stick". If you wish to visit, it is not too far from Medicine Hat, which this historian thinks would have been a much more suitable name. Keep your eyes open for stampeding buffalo, and keep your hands "stick-free." If your name is "Hank", just stay away. Buffaloes have long memories.

The First People soon discovered that the buffalo was a very useful animal, and not just for food. Tools, clothes, and ceremonial items could be formed from the remains of the magnificent creature. The First Nations People even used their (the buffaloes') dung as fuel for fires. Nothing like a good, juicy steak simmered over a pile of dung provided by the animal you are eating. Since irony hadn't been invented yet, it escaped the notice of the First Peoples, who nevertheless went on to create many tribes and nations in North

America, such as the Cree, the Sioux, the Dene, and the Chicago Blackhawks.

Although there were some conflicts between certain tribes, the majority of Native peoples were fairly decent to each other. This was due, in no small part, to the fact that there were so many resources, such as wood, food, and wi-fi coverage, that there were few reasons to fight and die. This is not to say that there were no confrontations at all, but cooler heads tended to prevail and conflicts were fewer than what the Europeans enjoyed.

💬 CLASSIC CANADIAN CONVERSATION

(Throughout the book there will be conversations that have captured a particular moment in Canadian history. Please note that these conversations have been painstakingly translated from my original chicken-scratching penmanship to the typed font you are now enjoying.)

NATIVE MAN: Hey! They have access to 143,521,732 buffalo! That's two more than our herd! Let's get 'em!
NATIVE WOMAN: Shut up and add more dung.

Yes, it was a peaceful time, but it wasn't to last.

STUDY QUESTIONS

1. DO YOU SHOP ON BOXING DAY?
2. WHO DO YOU THINK FIRST SET FIRE TO BUFFALO DUNG?
3. WHY DOESN'T 'MEDICINE HAT' SOUND FUNNIER THAN IT DOES?

CHAPTER TWO
THERE GOES THE CONTINENT

Since North America was so full of life and promise, it acted as a natural magnet for the Europeans who needed to steal and destroy in order to survive. (Their buffalo ran out many years before.)

The first group to visit was the Vikings. Vikings were a driven people because they owned only what they stole from less fortunate people, not unlike corporations today. The oldest sons of European families would get everything from Dad, so any other kids had to find their own way. Since pillaging your own town was frowned upon, (in the form of axes and arrows), the younger siblings tended to hop into boats and sail away, in the hopes of meeting other people whom they could pillage.

These intrepid voyagers would set sail from their lands and head west, since going east would mean running into your older brothers, who would arrow you to pieces. The boats were fairly small, so the Vikings were limited as to what they could bring with them, although it was still less restrictive than Air Canada.

Soon, the Vikings were settling places like Iceland (lush and green) and Greenland (mostly ice). The names seem a bit off, but no one said the Vikings were professors, and they were determined to get their piece of the Viking pie.* Led by Leif "Ramming Speed"

*Tastes as good as it sounds.

HOW THE VIKINGS SAID "GOODBYE" TO EUROPE

HOW THE VIKINGS SAID "HELLO" TO NORTH AMERICA

Ericsson, they found themselves in North America, and soon discovered how plentiful the New World was. The Vikings wanted to settle in Minnesota, but thought it too cold, so they relocated to the balmy shores of Newfoundland.

Once there, they set up a small village and set out to make a new life. They had their first contact with the locals, called the Beothuk, and the two groups tried some rudimentary trading. It it was far from easy, as we see in this:

CLASSIC CANADIAN CONVERSATION

> **NATIVE:** I'll give you three deer hides for that hammer.
>
> **VIKING:** I was thinking more like... (hits Native on head with hammer)
>
> **NATIVE:** Okay, four hides.
>
> **VIKING:** Hey, Sven. Show him how your battle-axe works.

This sort of misunderstanding was common in those days, and negotiations broke down quickly. The Vikings were vastly outnumbered, (and were also pretty ticked at being called the "Second Peoples") and the Natives knew all of the local geography and wildlife, so there really was only one option for these European visitors:

SVEN: We need to wipe out all these First Peoples.

Try as they might, the Vikings were simply too few, and although they had advanced weapons, they didn't have the foresight to bring smallpox (see Chapter Three) and had to leave North America in disgrace, sort of like an 11th century Conrad Black.

Some people doubt that the Vikings made it here so long ago, but we have proof of this! Archaeologists have determined that the Vikings were the first Europeans to visit North America because of a site in Newfoundland called "L'Anse aux Meadows", or, literally, "Answer the Meadows". How do they know it's a Viking site from over 1,000 years ago? They identified the following buildings: homes, workshops, a bathhouse, a kiln, and an Ikea. Also, they found a Viking wool-spinning tool, which proves that they brought some women along with them.*

STUDY QUESTIONS

1. WHAT'S THE DEAL WITH AIRLINE BAGGAGE FEES, ANYWAY?
2. IS THREE DEER HIDES A FAIR PAYMENT FOR A HAMMER?
3. SVEN SURE SOUNDS LIKE A JERK, EH?

---

*Although this sounds sexist, it really isn't meant to be. Viking men simply didn't do those chores deemed "for women." Please note that all of those Viking men are now dead. 21st Century men – you have been warned.

CHAPTER THREE
YOU CAN RELAX NOW –
THE WHITE MAN IS HERE!

The Native people of Newfoundland had dodged a bullet (arrow) when the Vikings left, and North America was left in peace by the Europeans for about 500 years.

As luck would have it, a plucky Italian explorer by the name of Christobal Colon decided to ask the Spanish King and Queen to finance his voyage *west* to find the Far *East*.* Anyway, ol' Christobal had spurned his native land, so he also changed his name to Christopher Columbus. (And 'Columbus, Ohio' sounds a lot better than 'Colon, Ohio'.) Well, the Spanish monarchy decided to fully fund his voyage, mainly because they were sick of hearing about how the world was round, and sent him off in the hopes of having him sail off the edge. Unfortunately for them, (and many others), Columbus didn't sail off the edge, but ran smack into some islands in the Caribbean and promptly claimed the whole place for Spain.

The local First Nations, called the Arawak, quickly retaliated to the theft of their land by presenting Columbus with many gifts of food, ceremonial items, and carved treasures. Columbus could

---

*Europeans were doing a lot of crazy things at this time. If you remember, ask me about the expedition to the bottom of the ocean to find the world's tallest goat.

EUROPEAN EXPLORATION

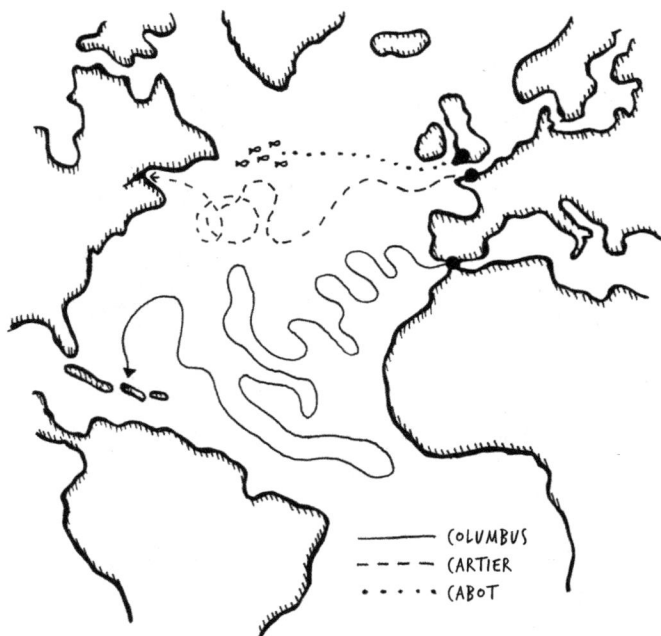

———— COLUMBUS
– – – – CARTIER
• • • • • CABOT

not abide this wanton display of 'nice', so he grabbed a few of the Arawak and headed back to Spain, but not before taking any gold he could find and paying for it with smallpox.

After Columbus's trip, everyone in Europe knew that there was another world out there – one full of beauty, mystery, and gold. Actually, not much gold had been brought back, but the stories of mountains of the stuff ensured that many Europeans would climb aboard boats and die somewhere in the Atlantic Ocean. The ones who made it were fortunate enough to die on land, and the really lucky ones only got scurvy and had all of their teeth fall out.

One of the earliest explorers was an Italian (like Colon), but sailed for the English. His English name was John "The *T* is Silent"

Cabot, translated from his Italian name, "Papa John's". When Columbus was looking for a route to the Orient, he took a direct, westerly route. Since the Earth is round, and he travelled near the middle part, it was also the "longest" or "stupidest" route. Cabot, not wanting to also be stupid, steered a bit more northerly, also known as "up". His trip was a bit shorter, but also colder, since he went into the North Atlantic Ocean – "Birthplace of the Iceberg". But before he made landfall, his ship ran into fish. Tons and tons of fish. The fish were so thick that his boat got stuck in them. Captain Cabot ordered the men to catch some fish for supper. Since 15th century sailors weren't the sharpest knives in the drawer, they threw, instead of nets, buckets over the side. Luckily for them, 15th century fish were also a bit dense and jumped right into the buckets. The sailors filled the boat with fish (and one surley mermaid) and headed home.

Cabot returned to England without gold, but he was the proud owner of the smelliest ship in the Atlantic. The King was happy with the fish, since most of England was eating moss, but what he really wanted was gold. So, he sent Cabot back with five ships this time, but they were never heard from again. People debate as to what happened to them, but it seems obvious to this historian that the billions of cod stopped their boats, rode up in the buckets, and ate the sailors.

The next serious explorer after Cabot was Jacques Cartier. He was a French sailor, but, in a twist of fate, he sailed for the French. Happy that he didn't have to change his name, Jacques set sail for the New World. By the time he got to where the fish had stopped Cabot's boats, European fishing fleets had already begun an aggressive "let's catch all the fish until there's nothing left" campaign – a noble tradition that continues to this day.

With few fish to challenge him, Cartier sailed up the St. Lawrence River and made landfall near an Iroquoian village called Quebec City. He immediately claimed the land for the King of France, "Frenchie the First". The Native chief, Donnacona, was pretty ticked at this, so Cartier, acting in the thoughtful and diplomatic manner that Europeans prided themselves on, kidnapped the Chief's two sons and took them back to France.

Well, King Frenchie wasn't too impressed with the non-gold-bearing Natives that Cartier had brought, so he sent him back with the kidnapped Natives and the instructions to return with gold. When Cartier arrived at the village with Donnacona's two sons, the locals remembered his treachery and weren't very happy with him. Their response was to threaten to cut the maple syrup candy shipment in half. Cartier had little choice but to kidnap the Chief himself, along with four more Natives. When the villagers tried to barter with Cartier for Donnacona's life by trading five others, Cartier kidnapped them, too. It was like free delivery.

Cartier took his ten 'guests' back to France where nine of them died in short order, including the Chief. The only survivor was a woman, and she never returned to her homeland. Cartier went on a third voyage to Canada, but instead of bringing back captives, which were quite worthless to the King, he brought back a few tons of fool's gold and quartz, which were quite worthless to the King. In his defense, he thought they were real gold and diamonds, and just because he couldn't tell the difference doesn't mean he's an idiot.*

Cartier never returned to Canada, so his total contribution to France's exploration of the New World was worthless rocks and

*Well, it does, but calling people names isn't very Canadian, eh?

dead Natives. He did manage to map the St. Lawrence, which opened up the continent and allowed more Europeans to come try their hand at settling the land, much to the delight of the Native North Americans.

♛ MEANWHILE, IN AMERICA...

This book is about Canada and the stories that took place in and around this great land, but we would be remiss if we ignored the U.S. Our two countries share a great deal of history, and although we don't see eye-to-eye on everything, it is safe to assume that we all agree that William Shatner was the best Captain of the U.S.S. Enterprise.

While we remain focused on Canada, we will periodically pause to consider what was happening in the U.S. of A., or what would become the U.S. of A. As Pierre Elliot Trudeau said of America, "Living beside you is like sleeping with an elephant. You steal all the blankets."

On that note, here is the first installment of:

♛ MEANWHILE, IN AMERICA...

At this time of frantic exploration of what would become the eastern coast of Canada, the future site of the U.S. of A. wasn't seeing much European action. Various Native groups were enjoying the last few years of peace and smallpox-free existence, but the trickles of Dutch, British, Spanish, and French settlers promised to disturb their way of life.

STUDY QUESTIONS

1. WOULD YOU GO TO THE COLON DAY PARADE?
2. IS "FRENCHIE" A GOOD NAME FOR A KING?
3. HOW ABOUT "FRANNIE"?

CHAPTER FOUR
THE WHITE MAN JUST WON'T GIVE UP

In 1604, a Frenchman named Pierre de Monts (literally, "Mountain Pie"*) tried to settle in the area of present-day southwestern Nova Scotia. He figured it would be a beautiful place to set up a permanent French settlement, mainly because the degree of latitude was the same as southern France and its topless beaches.

WHAT TO WEAR AT 44° LATITUDE DURING THE WINTER

OPTIONAL →

IN FEBRUARY
IT IS HIGHLY
RECOMMENDED
THAT YOU ALSO
WEAR ONE
ADULT MOOSE
IF POSSIBLE

IN FRANCE

IN NEW WORLD

*Tastes worse than Viking Pie.

After the first 12 feet of snow fell, Pierre realized that something was amiss. His men quickly set about getting scurvy and dying. And, if the snow and lack of oranges weren't bad enough, the local First Nations people, called the Maliseet, were a constant threat. (Actually, the threat was nonexistent, but after Cartier's stupidity, the French had ample reason to worry.) In fact, the Maliseet wanted to warn the French that the bay would soon freeze over and wreck their boats, but the French answered this warning with cannon fire. The Maliseet left and the French resumed their dying.

TYPES OF DEATH IN EXLPORATION OF "THE NEW WORLD"

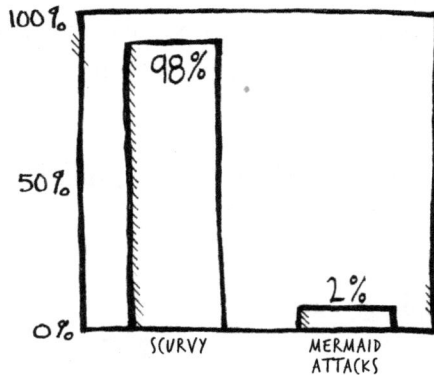

A young man named Samuel de Champlain ("Some Champagne, Sam") was with de Monts and learned some very valuable lessons on how to NOT run a settlement. He returned as a commander three years later, but, having remembered the horrific snow and cold of their previous attempt, decided to settle further north. (Champlain wasn't the brightest guy, but he had moxie.) In fact, he and his 27 men settled in the same area that our buddy Cartier had attempted to settle some 70 years before. Fortunately, for Champlain, Cartier's gift of smallpox had caused a widespread plague that almost wiped out the local populations and caused a war in the entire region. By the time Champlain showed up, the area was fairly deserted and the remaining tribes had no stomach for a fight.

Champlain's small settlement survived the winter, and by "survived" we mean that only 20 of the 28 men died. This was considered a smashing success by European settlement standards of that era. If it happened today, the government would have a solemn ceremony, then hire a private firm (owned by the PM's nephew's buddy) to investigate how it happened and who was at fault. When the finger of blame pointed back at the government, the investigation would be cancelled due to budget cuts.

Many Europeans still believed that there was a way to get through this annoying New World to get to the treasures of the Far East, so they continued to try. After Champlain there were others who followed: Frobisher, for England; Hudson, for England; Guy, for England...it appears to this historian as though the French figured there was no way to get to Asia by going west, so they spent their time and money sending many boatloads of settlers to settle the settlements. And, by 'settle', we mean 'get scurvy and die'.

♛ MEANWHILE, IN AMERICA...

Change was slow in coming to this area of North America. There was a small English colony that was formed. It was named Jamestown, after the leader, John Smith, and was located in present-day Virginia. Although they wanted to "show those Frenchies" how to settle properly, they too got scurvy and died. Hardly original, but enough people (two) survived the first winter to encourage England to send more settlers over and sink their claws into the fertile soil of the New World.

STUDY QUESTIONS

1. WHICH WOULD YOU RATHER EAT — VIKING PIE OR MOUNTAIN PIE? WHY?
2. HAVE YOU HAD SCURVY?
3. HOW ABOUT RICKETS?

CHAPTER FIVE
COLONIALISM REARS ITS UGLY REAR

A lot of books these days tend to heap derision on the colonial settlements in the New World. They talk about the disease, starvation, and fights with local Native tribes. They brand the colonists as some sort of blood-thirsty, war-mongering fools who brought misery to North America. Those books are correct. But this book will not simply follow suit. We will also talk about the lies, corruption, and stupidity of the colonists, although the settlers cannot take all the blame. "Attitude reflects leadership" is a great quote today, but if you uttered it back then, the 'leadership' would put your head on a pike. It is safe to assume that the Monarchy of each European country is to blame for most of the problems in the fledgling colonies, and the reason it is safe is that all those kings and queens are dead, and we don't see any pikes nearby.

Although England, Spain, and Holland were eager to get permanent settlements in North America, the French "took the cake"* in terms of settling the northern portion of the continent. By 1663 (actually, let's say 1666 – it's easier to remember) the French had established a Royal Colony at Quebec City. Since this vast area was to be ruled entirely by the King and his minions, they had to think of a catchy name. After much deliberation, more

*And ate it, too.

NORTH AMERICA 1600'S

arguing, and even more red wine, the sage leaders of France settled on the visionary name of this new French colony: "New France". It boggles the mind.

Since the new colony was on the St. Lawrence River (named after the first European man to discover it – Cartier) each farmer was given a long strip of land that reached from the river to far back into the woods. This system of land management was run by the Seigneur, so it was called "The King Said So" system. The Seigneur was the local landlord who, if he didn't die of scurvy, would ensure that all the farmers kept to their own land, paid taxes, and made the area profitable for the King. It worked pretty well, and New France began to grow.

The King decided that the Seigneurs needed a boss closer to home, so he invented the position of "Intendant". The first Intendant of New France was Jean Talon, who had a very cool last name. As Intendant, Jean was to ensure that the colony prospered and that people quit dying of scurvy. One of the better ideas Talon had came to him as he walked throughout the colony and noticed that most of the people were men. Although a few of the settlers had brought their wives with them, most had arrived alone hoping to find love in the New World, perhaps with a beautiful, non-smallpox-ed Native girl. Talon began a program to bring more than 1,000 eligible girls from France to New France to help populate the colony, and give the single males something to do besides cling to survival. These girls were called "Les Filles du Roi" which literally means "Royal Fillies", which gives you an idea as to how they were perceived in Old France.

But they married the local men quickly, since a failure to do so meant a return trip to France in shame, via canoe.

🏆MEANWHILE, IN AMERICA...

The English were settling an area now known as New England (original, eh?), but they first called it "New France" with the hopes of getting a few boatloads of those French girls dropped off closer to home.

New France grew into a respectable colony, and the locals were proud of the hard work and suffering they had endured. Although the people were not thought of too highly back in the home country, that all changed when the settlers started hauling dead beavers out of the woods. The beaver pelts were sent back to Europe and soon everyone wanted a beaver hat. It was warm and waterproof, and all the rage at snooty parties. Unfortunately,

EARLY BEAVER HATS

the beavers were becoming harder to find, so the French sent out trappers calling "Où étes-vous, castor? Castor! Castor!" As this didn't work at all, they turned to the First Nations people, who, after their laughter had died down, showed the French how to do it properly. Furs flowed for France. (Alliteration always amplifies...stuff.)

England, never wanting to play second fiddle, set out to get furs, too. They had a different system in mind, and instead of going out with the Natives to get the beaver pelts, they told them to get the furs and bring them to the trading posts. This didn't go over as well with the Natives, but they eventually reached an agreement:

💬ANOTHER CLASSIC CANADIAN CONVERSATION!

> **BRITISH TRADER:** Go get the furs and bring them back to this fort.
>
> **NATIVE:** But French come with us. Easier for us.
>
> **BRITISH TRADER:** I say, have you seen our cannon?
>
> **NATIVE:** How many ya' want?

Some may pass judgement on the English for making the First Nations trappers deliver the furs, while the French actually moved in with the Natives and learned their language and culture. One must remember, though, that the French way of doing things wiped out entire populations with diseases to which the locals had no immunity. The English were snobby, to be sure, but at least the First Nations lived long enough to see their land get taken from them. (See Chapter Thirteen.)

So the great Fur War of 16-something to 17-something went on and on, providing Europe's great empires with lots of gold and dry heads. It is possible that this conflict should be covered in much more detail, and many historians with their fancy degrees would say that it was the economic and political focus of Europe and deserves much more attention.

Luckily, for you, I'm choosing to ignore them.

STUDY QUESTIONS

1. WHY ELSE WOULD YOU 'TAKE A CAKE' BUT TO EAT IT, TOO?
2. WHY SECOND "FIDDLE"? WHY NOT SECOND "TUBA"?
3. AREN'T HISTORIANS ANNOYING?

CHAPTER SIX
THE WAR THAT SPAWNED TWO NATIONS (AND KILLED A FEW OTHERS).

Although there were many skirmishes between the English, the French, and the Native allies on both sides, full-blown war in North America wasn't realized until the English and the French decided to have a full-blown war in Europe.

Over the pond, England was fighting France, who was fighting Holland, who was fighting Spain, who was fighting Italy, who was fighting Portugal, who had no idea how to fight a war and decided to settle in Brazil, which was pretty peaceful except for the 100-foot snakes.

Naturally, all this unrest had to spill over to North America. The English and French were the only two European powers still fighting over 'Canadian' soil, with the French holding a huge advantage in number of soldiers, territory, and Native allies. Although the English had claimed a massive swath of land in the North, it only had a few hardy fur traders, most of whom lived on Hudson Bay. Seeing as how they lived on Hudson Bay, and built a strong economy on the shores of Hudson Bay, they formed a company that has become an icon of the Canadian retail landscape: Canadian Tire.

The rest of the English interests lay south of the St. Lawrence River in what was known as the "Lucky Thirteen" Colonies. They far outnumbered the French in North America, but most were simple farmers and tradespeople. Then King George the Somethingth sent a few thousand red coats over to help defeat the French. The people weren't sure what to do with so many coats until the King told them to put them on and shoot at the French people.

This strategy didn't work out too well, and the French won most of the battles in the first years of the war. Eventually, the war in Europe drew to a close (England won in overtime) and the British were able to send actual soldiers to North America. Soon after they arrived, they put on the red coats and began to shoot at the French soldiers. The people of New England were happy to let real soldiers do the fighting, and the tide turned in their favour.

The French may not have done well in the European war, but they did know how to build fortresses in the New World. They built a huge fortress called Louisburg on what is now Cape Breton Island. It was so massive and expensive that the French King Louis the Next wrote in his diary, "I shouldn't have eaten the clams." But the French were determined to ensure their continued dominance

SIZE COMPARISON

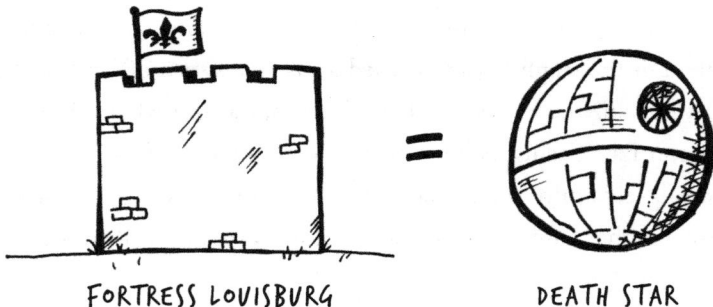

FORTRESS LOUISBURG   DEATH STAR

over the area, and this fortress would certainly do that! They built it on the coast and put a bajillion cannons on the walls to annihilate any English ships that were stupid enough to attack from the sea.

Believing that an attack could only come from the water, the French placed a grand total of zero cannons facing the land behind the fortress. They did place a sentry by the name of Henri there, and gave him a sharp stick, just in case. Of course, the British noticed this and decided that instead of attacking through a storm of cannonballs, they would take on Henri and his stick, pointy though it was.

The British won the day, and the French lost the fort. Shortly after, though, the British gave Louisburg back to the French in exchange for some land in India, which the French had taken previously. The King was quoted as saying, "They've got tea, wot!"

So, the French were happy to get their fortress back, and they promptly set about getting it ready by placing a bajillion cannons back on the walls. But they weren't about to make the same mistake twice! Since they learned that they were vulnerable from a land attack, they placed *all* their cannons facing towards that direction. On the water side, Henri was now equipped with a sharp stick *and* a rock. Of course, the British noticed this and attacked from the sea, and took the fortress again. This time, however, the British utterly destroyed the fortress, just in case the French may have actually learned how to defend it the next time.

One of the most pivotal battles of the conflict was the Plains of Abraham, which took place just west of Quebec City and east of Jerusalem. It was pivotal because in the book *How to Describe Battles*, it is stated in chapter 3, paragraph 9, subsection 83, appendix 2, that "the Battle of the Plains of Abraham shall be described as 'pivotal'".

PLAINS OF ABRAHAM

QUÉBEC CITY

NOVA SCOTIA

PLANES OF ABRAHAM

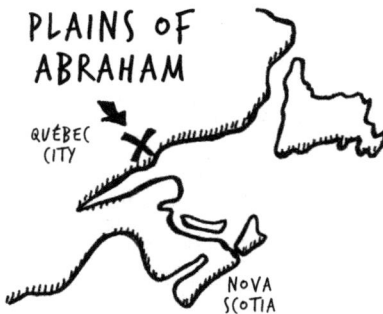

The actual battle only lasted a few minutes, and the two generals, James "The Fox" Wolfe (English), and Louis "We Gotta Go" Montcalm (not English), were both killed. Back in France, when the king finally heard about the defeat*, he was so depressed he tried to cheer himself up by purchasing another fine wig and some extra-tight pants, as was the style at the time. But the king remained mired in despair and tucked himself away in the corner of the palace which, in square footage, was similar to Africa.

Some folks tried to put a positive spin on things. The French philosopher Voltaire said that the loss of Canada wasn't to be dwelt upon, for it was only "a few acres of snow." A lesser-known philosopher named Wattaire added, "and pesky beavers, too". But the damage was done, and France simply licked her wounds and skulked back across the Atlantic.**

In those days, the governments of conquering nations tended to treat the losers with all sorts of disrespect and malice (as opposed to today, where governments treat their *own* people like this). But

---

*8 months later

**France still held two tiny islands just south of Newfoundland called St. Pierre and Michelob. Some people argue that this was a mistake, and could have opened the door to a rebirth of French colonization in North America. These people are what we call 'dumb'.

Britain was rather magnanimous towards the conquered French, mainly because there were 70,000 French and only a handful of British. They wrote up the Québec Act of 1774 which can be summed up easily: "Hey, Québec, as long as you don't take up arms against the Crown, you can have whatever you want from us. Freedom of religion, civil law, and inventing poutine can all be yours. And, even if you do revolt, we'll forgive you and continue to dole out money and perks to you from now until forever. Don't worry; the Thirteen Colonies have lots of cash, so we'll just tax them more. Cheers!"

Britain was now firmly in control of all of North America, except for the Spanish territories which included everything west of the Mississippi River. Britain had no more wish to fight another European power, so they told Spain to enjoy itself, but to stay there and behave, please. Unbeknownst to Britain, the Spanish were in the middle of a 100-year siesta.

♛ MEANWHILE, IN AMERICA...

The young colonies were pretty cheesed-off at Mom England. The war had cost Britain a ton of cash, but instead of taxing the people close to home, King George III decided to tax the colonials. This was done on such things as stamps, tea, sugar, cell phones, etc. Eventually, the colonists (let's call them 'Murricans') got so fed up they removed themselves from the yoke of Great Britain by riding around with feathers in their caps and other such crazy things. But more on that in Chapter Seven.

STUDY QUESTIONS

1. DO YOU FEEL SORRY FOR HENRI?
2. HAVE YOU EVER WORN TIGHT PANTS? HOW TIGHT? EXPLAIN.
3. DON'T YOU WISH WE HAD SIESTAS?

CHAPTER SEVEN
'MURRICA BUSTS OUT!

This chapter is dedicated to the birth of the United States of America. It was pretty messy, so bring a mop.

The American Colonies had been very prosperous. They took raw materials and sent them back to England, who turned them into consumer goods like chairs, doors, and toilets, and then sent them back to the Colonies with price tags attached. The colonists weren't too happy about the arrangement, so they decided to build their own factories and make their own toilets.

Although the vast majority of the colonists were descendents of Mother England, they had lived in North America for so long that they had lost their comical British accent and replaced it with a number of even more comical American accents. For example:

BRIT: I say, it appears as though we are in for a spot of rain before tea, wot!

AMERICAN: Dang it. That there cloud right there done look like it's a-bringin' some wet a-fore grub!

(Meanwhile, in Canada...)

CANADIAN: Snow, eh?

Now, the war between England and France had cost King George III a pretty farthing. (See chart below) Of course, he wanted his money back, but it was an election year and he didn't want to upset the local voters, so he decided to get his money from the colonies in the form of taxes. These taxes were pretty horrific, almost reaching the same level as the average Canadian taxpayer today, and the colonists felt bullied by the Crown. Not only did the taxes come crashing down on them, the King passed a law decreeing that Americans had to refer to football as "soccer". This was just too much, and action had to be taken!

UNDERSTANDING BRITISH MONEY IN ONE EASY CHART
(WITH CANADIAN CONVERSIONS)

ONE PENNY = FARTHING	A CANADIAN NICKEL
ONE FARTHING = 1/3 GUINEA PIG	A LOONIE
ONE GUINEA PIG = 1/7 CROWN	A LITRE OF MAPLE SYRUP
ONE CROWN = 4 TUPPENCE	WINNIPEG JETS TICKETS (SCALPED)

Some of the more influential colonists sprang into action. They were John Adams, George Washington Carver, brothers Thomas and George Jefferson, and Benedict "Eggs" Arnold. These men got together and wrote a letter stating that they wanted out of their relationship with Mother England. It was called, "The Declaration of Incontinence". The message was so important, and everyone so strongly agreed that it needed to be heard by the King, that they decided to put it behind glass and leave it in the museum. Since it was 1776, it took forever to write and was written with words that we *never* use anymore, like: "usurpations", "perfidy", and "Oldsmobile". If it were written today, it probably would have been an email that sounded like this:

Hey Britain, look, it's not working out, and I think we need some time apart. Face it, you've done some pretty bone-headed things, and my friends think you're kinda weird. Deep down, I think I still like you, but we live too far apart and we always go Dutch on dates. Gotta run. My shift at Burger King started ten minutes ago.

Keep it real,
The Colonies.

P.S. I pawned the ring.

Well, Britain wasn't too thrilled about the breakup, and decided to send a bunch of red coats over, this time with actual soldiers in them. They also hired some mercenaries called "Hessians", who were obviously from Germany. The King figured this would get those crazy colonies back in line, and he returned to his regular routine of figuring out how to tax the colonies some more. I mean, someone had to pay for all those soldiers, right?

Now, it must be said that not everyone in the colonies wanted to fight Mother England. According to some historical writings I read somewhere (instant oatmeal packages?) about one-third wanted to fight, one-third stayed loyal to the Crown, and one-third just wanted to sit this one out and join the side of whomever won, sort of like Calgary Flames fans.

The one-third who stayed loyal to the Crown didn't fare so well and were run out of town by the ones who wanted to fight. This one-third of loyal people were called "Loyalists", since imaginations hadn't been invented yet. As with all conflicts, tempers flared, and some nasty things were done on both sides. Many of the people who rebelled, called "Rebels", (didn't see

AMERICAN REVOLUTION

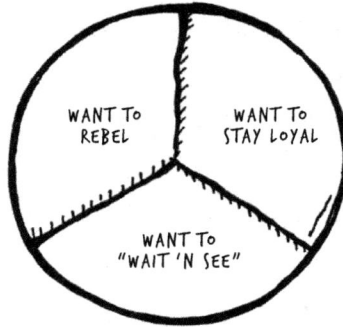

(NOTE THE HANDY PEACE SYMBOL USED IN THE DIAGRAM)

that one coming, did ya'?) did so because they believed it was fair payback for what the Crown had done to them for years. In truth, everyone was under the same oppressive system, but different people react differently. Some events seemed as unnecessary as a BLT at a bar mitzvah, as we can see in the actual conversation below:

REBEL: We're burning yer house down!

LOYALIST: Why?

REBEL: 'Cause England taxes us unfairly!

LOYALIST: But *I* don't tax you. In fact, I get taxed the same as you do.

REBEL: Uh...well...then we're burning yer house down 'cause you talk gooder!

Many things were done that would make Joseph Stalin look like Mother Teresa, but it was a difficult time for everyone. Eventually, the colonists won their independence on Independence Day, thanks

'MURRICAN SPEAK

ENGLISH: HELLO
'MURRICAN: HOWDY

ENGLISH: GOODBYE
'MURRICAN: SEE YA'

ENGLISH: I SAY, DO YOU HAVE THE TIME?
'MURRICAN: GIMMEE YOUR WATCH.

ENGLISH: I SAY, THAT'S NOT CRICKET
'MURRICAN: AND YOUR WALLET.

to the steely resolve of Will Smith, Jeff Goldblum, and a semi-sober Randy Quaid. Before the end of the conflict, thousands of colonists and their families had moved away. Most came to Canada, but some headed back to England. Still others went to British islands in the Caribbean and opened up beach side restaurants with swim-up bars. There was no denying that a new nation had been formed as a result of the American Revolution, but it must also be noted that the mass influx of Loyalist settlers to British colonies in the north laid the foundation for the formation of another country just a short 84 years later. (Spoiler Alert!) It was Canada.

STUDY QUESTIONS

1. WHAT'S YOUR FAVOURITE ACCENT?
2. HAVE YOU BEEN TO A BAR MITZVAH?
3. DID YOU READ PAST THE "SPOILER ALERT"? WHY?

CHAPTER EIGHT
THE WAR NOBODY WON (EXCEPT CANADA)

Ask a Canadian about the War of 1812 and you'll undoubtedly hear something like this: "It was the first war here on Canadian soil, and we won!" Unfortunately, there are a couple of mistakes: one, it wasn't the first war fought on this soil, as the American Revolution had a number of battles here; and, two, Canadian soil didn't exist yet, at least not as we know it today. It was, technically, British soil, but less pretentious. The term "we won" is also suspect as most of the fighting was done by British troops, but, you gotta love the attitude, eh?

Ask an American about the War of 1812 and you'll undoubtedly hear something like this: "Is that where we dropped them nukes on y'all?" No, seriously, most Americans don't know about this war for a simple reason – they didn't win it, so they don't teach it in school. I have some great American friends who are quite learned (two syllables) and even they shy away from discussing the War of 1812, sort of like not wanting to discuss last year's Christmas party. (Mark, I'm looking at you...) In fact, for Americans, the War of 1812 and a crazy night out have a link: they both seemed like a good idea at the time.

Although the actual conflict took place in a fairly small area geographically, there were a number of people groups that need to be clearly recognized: the Americans, the British, the Natives (of which there were many different Nations), the Canadians, and the Canadiens. The last two appear to be the same, but are quite different. The *Canadians* were English-speaking farmers and business folk who had come from England and America to start

PROMINENT WAR OF 1812 "OUR SIDE" CHARACTERS

BRITISH — BROCK CHARGING THE CANONS

CANADIAN — LAURA SECORD WALKING TO WARN BRITISH OF AMERICAN AMBUSH

FIRST NATIONS — TECUMSEH RALLYING FIRST NATIONS TO BRITISH SIDE

CANADIEN — CHARLES DE LA SALABERRY DEFYING A MUCH LARGER AMERICAN FORCE

PROMINENT WAR OF 1812 "THEIR SIDE" CHARACTERS

FILE NOT FOUND

a new life and learn how to shovel snow properly. The *Canadiens* were a hockey team from Montréal.

Wars happen for all sorts of reasons, and this war had a pretty good reason for starting, but many don't know the real truth. Luckily for you, you are holding the unabashed, historically sound truth as to both the causes and outcomes of the conflict!*

The Royal Navy was the supreme ruler of the seas, and all those warships would hamper the growing trade between America and European countries, such as Paraguay. But the Brits also tried their hand at kidnapping, you know, to make up for the Revolution, wot! When they spotted an American ship, they would board it and arrest some sailors on the charge of being deserters from the Royal Navy. Of course, this was often a trumped-up offense, so the Americans, tired of being pushed around by England, decided to take action! Since attacking Britain directly was impossible, the Americans decided to invade their Canadian colony. What could be easier?

At this time, "Canada" was made up of two distinct regions: Upper Canada and Lower Canada, now known respectively as Ontario and France. There was also Atlantic Canada, but not much was happening there, a tradition that continues to this day. Most of the battles in the War of 1812 took place in Upper Canada, although a few crucial fights did take place in other areas, including American soil.

♔ MEANWHILE, IN AMERICA...

The Americans were still pretty choked up about not capturing Montréal and Québec during the American Revolution and figured now was a good time to strike. Plus, the Royal Navy was being a thorn in the country's collective side. Britain was once again embroiled in a war versus the French, and the Americans decided it was a good

*No, you're not.

*time to right those wrongs. The cry, "Manifest Destiny" went up, and,
since most Americans didn't know what it meant, the response was
underwhelming.* *

Since you were paying attention in the last chapter, you know
that many thousands of people living in Canada at this time had left
the Thirteen Colonies during the unpleasantness of the Revolution.
And after the Revolution, many thousands more came north to
enjoy the free farmland and clouds of mosquitoes. Also, since the
British tended to get along better with the First People, that area was
a much more peaceful place to settle. (Of course, this relationship is
something that has been lost along the way.)

Knowing that so many of the people residing in Upper Canada
were transplanted Americans, the leaders of the U.S. of A. figured
that they could just walk in and take it, and their troops would be
welcomed with open arms. In fact, Thomas Jefferson was quoted as
saying, "Taking Canada will be a mere matter of marching through
the tulips." Unfortunately for Tom and the boys, Canada had no
tulips at the time, so while the massive American army trudged
around looking for the flowers, Canadian militia and their Native
allies would sneak up behind them and hit them over the head
with hockey sticks.**

Well, this tactic worked for a while, but it was obvious that the
British Redcoats would have to do most of the fighting if Canada
were to remain "free", meaning, under the yoke of the English
Crown. Soon, the war bogged down into an endless stream of

*"Manifest Destiny" was the belief that the U.S. should govern all of North America, South
America, Africa, and parts of Greenland. It was the rallying cry of the politicians who
wanted nice places to spend their time during summer vacation, shooting large animals.

**This writer has been informed by Professor Google that hockey hadn't been invented
by this time. This writer disagrees.

battles until the Americans tired of the hockey violence and went back home to invent basketball.*

There were important battles on the Great Lakes also, and the Americans gained control of Lake Erie when their naval officer uttered the famous battle cry, "Don't shoot until you see the whites of their eyes!" Sadly, the British commander had instructed his men, "Don't shoot until you see the pinks of their uvulas!", and this confused the men to no end, allowing the Americans to close in and win the day.

One of the more famous stories from the War of 1812 tells of Laura Secord, a Canadian woman who married an American fellow who farmed the area where the Americans invaded. When the Americans used her house as their officers' quarters, she overheard their plans to attack a small British force nearby. Laura took action and made a bunch of chocolates for the American troops. While they were sleeping off their sugar high, she dramatically walked over 30 kilometres (1,000 miles) to warn the British, who then set an ambush and won the day. The American prisoners promised to never fight on our soil again, if they could please get a few boxes of chocolates for the road.

There were great victories and tactical blunders on both sides, but honestly, the Americans really didn't have their hearts in the fight. They outnumbered the British, Canadian, Canadien, and Native forces in every engagement, but couldn't handle the sheer ferocity of our fore-checking. In a desperate attempt to turn the tide of the war, the Americans pulled the goalie, but to no avail. The Americans did loot York (now called Toronto), but then British troops looted Washington (now called Washington) and burned half of the President's home, (now called the Pentagon).

*Invented by a Dr. James Naismith, a Canadian.

Looking at the Heroes of the War of 1812 gives us a glimpse of who celebrates the struggle more heartily: Sir Isaac Brock (British), Tecumseh (Native, allied with British), Charles de Salaberry (Canadien), and Laura Secord (Canadian). The heroes of the American side were...hmmm...well, there was that one guy who won one battle on Lake Erie. We'll try to find his name before the end of the chapter.

Okay, so most of the heroes were on the Canadian/British/Canadien/Native side, and most of the major engagements were won by the same. The Americans did win the Battle of New Orleans, and since it was such a rare thing, they wrote a song about it called "The Devil Went Down to Georgia". That particular battle actually happened two weeks after the end of the war, so it doesn't really count.

The most solid argument as to who won this war can be summed up in one question. Who ended up with the nicer part of Niagara Falls?

STUDY QUESTIONS

1. WOULD YOU RATHER HAVE CAKE OR POUTINE? EXPLAIN.
2. HAVE YOU SEEN YOUR UVULA RECENTLY? IS IT PINK?
3. DID YOU FIND OUT THAT AMERICAN NAVAL OFFICER'S NAME? WE DIDN'T.

CHAPTER NINE(A)
UNREST IN THE UPPER AND LOWER PARTS

The War of 1812 ended in 1814, and people on both sides of the border lived in relative peace with each other. Most of British North America was split into two main parts: Upper and Lower Canada. (There also existed Atlantic Canada, but they were really calm and pleasant, and we won't mention them in a chapter filled with violence and uppity-ness.)

We'll start with Upper Canada, now called Ontario.* The year was 1837. It was clear to everyone, including the 'Murricans, that these British colonies were here to stay. Thanks to a large amount of British help in the form of Redcoats and muskets, they had fought hard for their freedom, sacrificed a great deal over three years of war, and had enjoyed a peaceful existence since then. Roads and canals took produce to markets, the population grew rapidly, and things seemed almost utopian. Clearly, they now had no choice but to revolt against Great Britain.

Now, this revolt didn't happen overnight. It was a seriously planned, well-considered strategic move that would guarantee more autonomy for the fledgling colony. Below is a step-by-step recounting of those fateful days:

---

*Yes, it really is. We looked it up.

DAY ONE: March on the government buildings in Toronto to
demand better representation at the top levels of power.

DAY TWO: Surrender.

Unlike the American Revolution, this one was over with
very little bloodshed – in fact, almost none. It was Revolution:
Canadian style.*

There were good reasons for this uprising. Upper Canada
was run by a system called The Family Compact. Although it
sounds like a nepotism-based system of government that had no
accountability to the people whatsoever, that's exactly what it was.

The revolt was led by William Lyon MacKenzie, the great-
great-great grandfather of that iconic future Canadian Prime
Minister, Joe Clark. He (not Clark) wanted to reform the
government so that it could be a stronger, more effective voice for
the people, namely, his friends. As the above day-by-day account
shows, they marched on the government in Toronto, hoping to
surprise the local garrison and take their guns, which are always
handy in a revolution.

On that crucial first (and second-to-last) day, Willie took
precautions. He dressed in a large number of overcoats that he
hoped would stop the musket balls that were certain to come his
way. Although the rest of the men were cheesed off at having to
give up their coats on that chilly December morning, they were
more distracted by the fact that most of them had pitchforks, not
muskets. They followed Willie anyway, who now looked less like a
leader of men than a leader of penguins.

---

*Some manuscripts, which are less-reliable than this one, say that the rebellion
took almost four days, but it's obvious to this historian that those stats are padded to
add drama.

W.L.M. LEADS REBELLION

"Charge!" cried the Penguin King, and the men ran down Yonge Street towards the handful of defenders who fired a volley and retreated. The few rebels with guns dropped down to return fire, but Willie thought they had been killed. "Retreat!" cried the Penguin King, and the revolution was pretty much over. He and his men trudged back to Montgomery's Tavern to drown their sorrows in a pint and watch the hockey game.*

The colonial government, having won the previous day with a mere five guys who fired once and ran away, decided to take it to the next level. They marched on the tavern with 600 militiamen, complete with cannons! (This sort of overkill by the Canadian government has been repeated on countless occasions, most notably when this historian was sent a tax adjustment notice for $1.43, which, after processing, printing, and shipping, cost them about $100.00. It's this type of thinking that killed the dinosaurs.) In any event, the revolutionaries, still suffering from too many pints the night before, were in no mood for a scrap. Willie, no longer

---

*The Leafs lost 4-1.

looking like a penguin, was fleet of foot and ran off to the States, hoping to gather up support for another attempt at overthrowing the government. Unfortunately for him, the Americans still remembered the drubbing from 1812 and weren't too keen on repeating it. So, William Lyon MacKenzie had no choice but to return to Upper Canada in disgrace.*

STUDY QUESTIONS

1. WHY DO THE LEAFS LOSE SO OFTEN?
2. DO YOU PAY YOUR TAXES?
3. WHAT DO YOU THINK KILLED THE DINOSAURS?

*By 'disgrace', we mean that he ended up being elected to the Upper Canada Legislative Assembly, which was utterly impotent in the face of the Family Compact. Irony runs thick in Canada.

CHAPTER NINE(B)
LE GRANDE NASTY

Whew. That last chapter was kind of fun, eh? Well brace yourself, because although Lower Canada didn't have the Family Compact, it did have the Château Clique. This may sound a bit classier, but it was pretty much just like the Family Compact with more red wine.

The rebellion in Upper Canada had been almost bloodless. The rebellion in Lower Canada (now called "Québec") was a bit less cheery. Remember, this colony was settled by the *Canadiens*, and they were nothing if not passionate. Their leader went by the name of Joseph "Pop" Papineau, who was a fantastic orator, and a decent sous-chef. He got the locals so whipped up against the government that they actually shot and killed *six* British soldiers!*

Unfortunately for the Canadiens, the British government decided to stomp on this uprising before the deaths got into double-digits. They sent over 1,000 Redcoats and a few hundred English-Canadian militia to quell the fledgling rebellion. And quell, they did. (More violence coming.)

There were a number of skirmishes, but the largest battle was also the final battle. It happened in St. Eustache and the British troops ended the rebellion by killing most of the rebels. Papineau

*Sorry for the violence. We'll warn you next time.

did what all good Canadians do when they are looking for a way out of their problems: he fled to the States.

♛ MEANWHILE, IN AMERICA…

The Americans were getting a little nervous about these 'peaceful neighbours' and all the uprisings. They were most fearful of losing their title as "rootin-est, shootin-est nation in North America", and set about preparing to have a civil war.

The Lower Canada Rebellion actually spanned a couple of years, and it included a number of raids from sympathetic Americans who still wanted the Brits gone. Of course, these raids were dismal failures and eventually petered out. (Or is it "Pierred" out?)

So, what was to be done? Britain certainly had a problem on her hands: two distinct populations living side-by-side, speaking different languages, with different Mother Countries, and different opinions on everything from religion to farming. It is perfectly obvious to us historians that this situation could lead to further revolutions. Surprisingly, it was also perfectly obvious to the old white guys in Britain, who usually missed these sorts of things because they were too busy inventing inedible food. But what could be done with these two strikingly different people groups living under the rule of England? What could be done to avert yet more unrest? Wait! I've got it!

Get them married to each other.

STUDY QUESTIONS

SEE CHAPTER NINE(A).
- WE FILLED OUR QUOTA OF THREE QUESTIONS PER CHAPTER, PLUS WE CAN'T THINK OF ANYTHING RIGHT NOW.

CHAPTER TEN
UNITED WE KNEEL

Great Britain, in all her wisdom, decided to make one big province out of two smaller ones. Upper Canada and Lower Canada would have all of their affairs 'united' under one provincial government and be called "The United Province of Canada".* This Act of Union was formally passed as the "Act of Opposites Attract" and at no point in history had there been so many people thinking, "I'll bet it doesn't last six months", with Jennifer Lopez weddings being a notable exception.

The marriage of these two very different colonies was about as smooth as sandpaper, mainly because all the guests brought similar wedding gifts. Things such as equal representation and honest leadership were ignored, and this upset Lower Canada trés much, since those gifts had been on the list when they registered at Eaton's. Upper Canada knew that she'd get everything she asked for since Daddy was paying for the reception.

Well, this "union" seemed to actually work out alright since there were no more rebellions like those in 1837, or, as we historians like to call it, Chapter Nine. Peace was realized, thanks in no small part to the bajillion Redcoats the British stationed in those well-known problem areas. Life gained some measure of normalcy for people living in the large British colony,

*At some point in history, you'd think that somehow, someone, somewhere, would come up with an original name for a newly-minted geo-political region. You'd be wrong.

and the money, food, and entertainment flowed freely. Land was beginning to open in the western part of the province, and European settlers began to trickle in.

Sometime during this period (1200 B.C.–1866 A.D.) a guy by the name of Egerton Ryerson dropped in from England in order to find out why the local children were so stupid. Having won the coveted "Wackiest First Name in England" trophy for the past five years, he was eager to come to this backwater colony. What he discovered was that our current education system was severely lacking an important piece of the educational puzzle – teachers. He quickly solved this by forming a university that has been synonymous with the great Mr. Ryerson ever since: Queen's University. He also implemented a lot of useful protocols such as: the strap, the whip, and the ever-popular 'board of education'. Although children weren't too happy about this, parents seemed thrilled at the idea of school. Of course, school only took place when children weren't needed on the farm, so the school 'year' was from November to March. You know those stories about walking to school in hip-deep snow? All true.

To be honest, not a lot of interesting stuff happened in the area during this time, or so our four-minute Google search told

CANADIAN CHILDREN WALKING TO SCHOOL
1865 OR SO...

us, anyway. There were some canals constructed, as well as some small railways, but the real building that happened was (drum roll, please)...the Building of a Nation! Yes, Canada, with her majestic mountains, snow-swept Prairies, and flooded Toronto basements, was almost a reality!

♕ MEANWHILE, IN AMERICA...

The U.S. Civil War was on. It was very unpleasant, and many soldiers died. It was fought along ideological lines, (Blue and Grey), and pitted brother against brother, uncle against grandfather, and nephew against second-cousin once removed. It took years to fight, and after it was all done things went pretty much back to how they were before, except President Lincoln freed all the slaves in those "mean and nasty" Southern states. (The ones in the North remained slaves, but they were called "servants", so it was okay.)

No, there wasn't any civil war in Canada, but it's not like people didn't have anything to complain about. Some people were upset that the roads had so many ruts in them, while others bemoaned the fact that the maple syrup wasn't quite as plentiful as the previous year.* With issues like these, you have to know that a major change was coming.

STUDY QUESTIONS

1. WHATEVER HAPPENED TO EATON'S?
2. WOULD YOU EVER NAME YOUR CHILD "EGERTON"? HOW ABOUT A PET?
3. NEITHER WOULD WE.

*It's similar to how Canadians complain today, except some want to know why there are so many pot holes in Winnipeg, while others want to know why the Leafs can't win.

CHAPTER ELEVEN
CONFEDERATION COMES HOME AT LAST!

Canada was birthed on July 1st, 1867, at 5:46 p.m. (local time), weighing 7 lbs 2 oz, and measuring just over 500 bajillion square kilometres in length.* The event was presided over by a number of old white guys with comical haircuts. Fortunately, Canada has advanced heroically since then, and now Canada is led by both men and women, old and young, of different ethnicities, many of whom have comical haircuts.

The ceremony took place in Charlottetown, Prince Eddie Island, and although PEI was invited to come along for the ride, they were so busy cleaning rooms and mixing drinks that they missed the signing. They also spent a lot of time complaining that the Federal Government probably wouldn't care about them after they were in the club, which proves PEI had the first fortune-tellers in Canada.

There were a great many issues to discuss before Confederation came into being: the railway across the country, the cost of national defense and who should pay for it, and whose face should go on the new Canadian money. The last point was argued for a goodly number of days, and although no consensus was immediately

*We apologize for mixing Imperial measurements with Metric, and also for using a measure of area to describe distance. We're just very emotional at birthings. Ask my wife.

reached, they took one look at the American money and said, "nope". Not only did Canada use different colours for each bill, they also added the letter "u" to "color", just to bug the Americans. At the end of the Confederation Conference, four provinces had agreed to join the new country called Canada. They were, in alphabetical order: Ontario, Québec, New Brunswick, and Nova Scotia. Since PEI felt shunned from the start, they short-sheeted the beds, which resulted in the other provinces leaving only a 5% tip. Ontario stole a bathrobe.

Since this is a history book, and history is full of people, we should probably tell you about some of the key figures at this event. There was our first prime minister, Sir John "Eh" Macdonald's, Sir Charles Tupperware, Willie "The Protestant" Pope, and John Johnson, who was voted to have the most boring name at the conference. These men presided over the fledgling nation's course and did a good enough job that other areas soon wanted to join up. More and more provinces came aboard, usually because of the promise of a railway, a common defense force, and the forgiveness of gambling debts. Below is the list of provinces and territories, the year they each joined, and their official mottoes:

1867 – Ontario: "Come see our air"
   Québec: "Je me souviens la recette pour la poutine"
   New Brunswick: "We need government assistance"
   Nova Scotia: "So do we"
1870 – Manitoba: "Just keep driving"
   Northwest Territories: "Come write your name in our snow"
1871 – British Columbia: "Ferry rates are up again"
1873 – Prince Edward Island: "We dig spuds"

1898 – Yukon Territory: "We wear plaid"
1905 – Alberta: "Home of the cracked windshield"
       Saskatchewan: "Flat, and plowed of it"
1949 – Newfoundland and Labrador: "Cod free since 1996"
1999 – Nunavut: "Where The Northern Lights are South"

LIKE ANY FINE MAPLE SYRUP, CANADA IS SWEET, THICK, AND EXPENSIVE

Thanks to Confederation, millions of people now enjoy freedom, a high quality of life, and some of the highest tax rates in the history of the planet. Yes, this nation of ours* has been the home to many scientific breakthroughs, social awareness breakthroughs, and road-repair breakthroughs that are the envy of all. Like the

*Canada

famous Statue of Liberty in New York, we welcome the huddled masses and downtrodden folk who are only looking for a better life for their family. We willingly accept all people, regardless of ethnicity, religion, or political stance, as long as they have money.

Now that Canada was an actual place, and needed to form a national identity, certain events were put in motion to make that identity become a reality. Events that would stir the soul and make people proud to call this great land their home. The events of which we speak are, of course, rebellions.

♟MEANWHILE, IN AMERICA...

The American Civil War was over, and the North, also known as the "Union", also known as the "Blue", also known as the "Yankees", also known as "The Side That Had Every Advantage But Still Took Forever To Win", had won. Now, instead of the nastiness of Civil War, where Americans were attacking Americans, the people could settle down and focus on what was really important – attacking "non-Americans", such as Native tribes, Mexicans, and Orientals.

STUDY QUESTIONS

1. DO PREFER THE METRIC SYSTEM?
2. GIVE 10 REASONS WHY.
3. EXPLAIN "HECTOMETRE".

CHAPTER TWELVE
CANADIANS BEHAVING BADLY

As Canada stretched out from her initial borders shortly after Confederation, she found herself bumping into established settlements with actual real people in them. One of the most notable cases revolved around present-day Winnipeg, Manitoba. The settlement in question was located at the forks of two rivers, the Red and the Assiniboine, and since the Red River was the main source of water, they called the settlement the "Red River Settlement". Wow.

Most of the settlers at the Red River Settlement were Métis. This was a growing group of hearty folk whose parents had been a combination of one French parent and one Native parent. Although in today's Canada this is not an issue, back then the Métis were looked upon with the same value as buffalo dung, only not as flammable.*

Wherever Métis went, they found that most others didn't accept them, so it was natural that they would form their own colony away from prying eyes and wagging tongues, and the Red River Settlement was made to do just that. They began to work the land and tame the wilderness area around them, and they created a nice little existence for themselves.

*See Chapter One

Now, if a prosperous colony existed near its borders, the new nation of Canada, with her shiny-new government, needed to either stop it or appropriate it. They went with option #2 and sent out land surveyors to chart all the land that seemed desirable for farming and development. In truth, the land they were surveying was mostly settled already, but it was done in a less "officious" manner. Witness a typical exchange in the early days of settlement:

💬A CLASSIC CANADIAN CONVERSATION!
(Translated from the original French, eh?)

MÉTIS 1: So, how's about I take this area 'round about here?

MÉTIS 2: Sounds fair. I'll take this land 'round about there.

MÉTIS 1: Yep. Should work out dandy.

MÉTIS 2: Sure for sure.

ENGLISH LAND SURVEYOR: Sorry, but I'm here to parcel up the land and give it to rich Eastern folks.

MÉTIS 1: Oh, I don't like the sound a that.

MÉTIS 2: You bet. Anyways, we already divvied it up, clean as you please.

ENGLISH LAND SURVEYOR: You did it wrong.

MÉTIS 1: How's that?

ENGLISH LAND SURVEYOR: You're Métis. You don't count.

MÉTIS 1: For sure we can. There's me, you, and Métis #2. That's three.

MÉTIS 2: Which one am I again?

Flare ups like this one could have been avoided if Ottawa simply quit sending out surveyors, but they continued to do so and the land was slowly surveyed to fulfill the East's desires. The surveyors would use carefully calibrated measurement chains to plot out the land and then auction off the land to rich folks back East, namely, railway owners. The railway bought all the fertile land around the area and left the swampy, rocky land for the Métis.

To protect the land they had worked for years, and to ensure their survival as an autonomous colony, the Métis acted swiftly, and without mercy. They erupted in an orgy of uncontrolled mayhem! It was chaos extramplified!* This bloodthirsty frenzy included all of the following actions:

1. They hid the surveyors' chains.

Peaceful Canada was shaken to its very core. It was madness like this that almost prevented Canadian expansion. This violent form of public insurrection had to be dealt with quickly, lest the fledgling federal government lose respect in the West! (cough)

☤MEANWHILE, IN AMERICA...
The U.S. 7th Cavalry was "escorting" a Native tribe off their ancestral land because they had the gall to speak a different language and ride horses without a saddle.

It was obvious to the government that this type of anarchy couldn't be dismissed, so action was taken! They decided to appoint a governor, William "Stubby" McDougall, to oversee the goings on in the Northwest Territory which was about 563 bajillion square

*My editor tells me this isn't a real word. What a lorganschpleckler.

miles and the Red River Settlement just happened to be smack-dab right in the middle.*

McDougall was anxious to get things settled in the settlement, so he showed up a few days early, but the Métis were ready for him! Over a dozen armed men blocked his attempt to get into the office. This event is often referred to by government officials as a reason to never, ever be *early* for work. Being an hour or two *late* is now the acceptable tactic used so that they never get blocked by armed Métis.

The Métis needed a leader. They scoured the land looking for a suitable candidate. They needed a rich, wise, urbane leader who could parry every thrust of the Prime Minister's Office and act on their behalf with a calm, charismatic charm. This man needed to exude a confidence and clarity not witnessed since King Solomon.

Having exhausted themselves looking for such a man, they decided to use the tried and true method of "hands up whoever wants to lead us in the fight against the federal government". One man who had arrived late at the meeting didn't know what was going on and raised his hand to ask. It was a defining moment for him, as the crowd lifted him on their shoulders and paraded around the room with their newfound, albeit confused, saviour: Monsieur Louis Riel.

There was one fellow who lived at the Red River Settlement who did support the Feds, and his name was Thomas Scott. He was an English-speaking guy who came to the area as a surveyor (remember them?) and stuck around after he found his chains and completed his work. Apparently, he wasn't the nicest person, and

*Actually, it wasn't even close to the middle, but why worry about facts this far into the book?

he even led an attack on the Métis fort that had been built to help protect the colony. The attack failed, so Riel had him tried as a criminal. Scott only spoke English, so Riel had his trial conducted wholly in French, which really sped up the proceedings. Acting as judge, Riel closed the trial with that famous French phrase, "Je suis faim. Donnez moi le poulet frit." Scott didn't understand the gravity of this, but soon he was in front of the firing squad and it all became quite clear. The last word he ever heard was "FEU!"*

Naturally, news of this reached back East and the English-speaking Canadians were quite upset. They pressured Sir John the Prime Minister to do something about it. And do, he did! He made Manitoba into a province. Now, since it was Canadian soil, he could protect it with Canadian troops. He sent 1,200 troops out there with the mandate to abduct Riel and bring peace to the area. Unfortunately, many of these young troops were illiterate, and the orders got a bit confusing at times. This opens the door to another...

💬 CLASSIC CANADIAN CONVERSATION!

SOLDIER 1: Hey, what did the sergeant say?

SOLDIER 2: He said we have a mandate to "abduct" Riel, eh!

SOLDIER 1: What does that mean?

SOLDIER 2: It means "shoot", eh!

The journey westward was fraught with trials and dangers, but they carried on and arrived three months later. With over 1,000 men, some cavalry, and even some cannons, this force was nothing to be ignored. Quickly, Riel reacted in a typically "Canadian leader bent on rebellion" manner to this action: he fled to the U.S.

*It means "DUCK!", but since Scott didn't understand French, he just stood there.

JUST LIKE MACKENZIE AND PAPINEAU, RIEL RUNS TO SAFETY!

U.S. BORDER

So, for those keeping score, the rebellions in Canada (or even soon-to-be Canada) were not finding much success and were 0-3 versus the governing power at the time. But now, Canada had five provinces under the guidance of Ottawa, and Canada seemed stronger than ever!

Uh-huh.

STUDY QUESTIONS

1. HAVE YOU EVER BEEN TO WINNIPEG?
2. I MEAN, IN THE DEAD OF WINTER?
3. DID YOU BUY A SLURPEE? I DID.

CHAPTER THIRTEEN
CANADA: EVERYONE IS WELCOME!
(UNLESS YOU WERE HERE FIRST)

As we have now seen, Canada was birthed and weaned in a fairly calm, quiet process, especially when compared to the U.S. Sure, there was some unrest beforehand, and a little rebellion here and there, but compared to many other nations, Canada was able to come into being rather peacefully.

Canadians are recognized around the world as being kind, caring, and thoughtful people, but it was not always so. No, we haven't always been the type of people to give you the poutine off our plate. In fact, when Canada was only a few years old, the leaders (remember, old white guys with funny haircuts) realized that there happened to be a large number of non-white folks living where rich white folks would like to settle and build railroads and time share condos. They (the old white guys) had witnessed some of the violence that erupted south of the border when Whites and First Nations 'discussed' who should live where, and they wanted to avoid that up here. But what could be done?

The old white guys met in Ottawa and gave themselves a strict timeline to complete this difficult task. They toiled day and night, refusing to rest until the work was done. They came up with a plan

CANADIAN GOVERNMENT 1870

WE'RE HERE TO LIVE
IN PEACE WITH ALL
PEOPLE WHO DO WHAT
THEY'RE TOLD!

that would bring about peace and prosperity for both sides, and ensure that settlers and First Nations would grow to understand and help each other become responsible citizens of this new land. The railway would be carefully surveyed, and its route would respect traditional Native grounds and also take care not to ruin land that was already settled by the locals. This plan was so wise in its content and succinct in its writing that it only took one page to write it! Unfortunately, all of the work was destroyed when one of the members accidentally dropped it in the hot tub.

Knowing that their time was just about exhausted, they quickly scrawled out some instructions on napkins and called them "Treaties". There were eleven Treaties in all, and the last one wasn't completed until 1921, far from any hot tubs. What did these Treaties say, exactly? Well, we're not sure of *all* the details*, but here's the gist:

GOVERNMENT	FIRST NATIONS
CAN CLAIM ANY TERRITORY WHICH LOOKS PROFITABLE IN ANY WAY, SHAPE, OR FORM.	GET TO MOVE OFF THE LAND BEFORE THE BULLDOZERS COME IN.

* Surprised?

Okay, it wasn't all that bad. The Government did give some money to help build communities, complete with casinos. And they did promise put a stop to the horrible liquor trade. (And, if they couldn't stop it, they'd at least tax it heavily. It's a win-win, right?)

The negotiations that followed the initial treaties were not always happy affairs. The Natives would accuse the government of using trickery and trinkets to rob their people of ancestral and sacred grounds, and they would contend that the government was being shady in their dealings and couldn't be trusted to carry out their promises. The government would respond that the Natives wore too much leather. In the end, the First Nations were simply too few and the government did what it wanted to do, anyway.*

Similar to a Toronto Blue Jays' season, the relationship between the Canadian government and the First Nations has seen some good moments, bad moments, and worse moments. In all honesty, the Jays aren't nearly as interesting.

STUDY QUESTIONS

1. WHY DID 19TH CENTURY WHITE GUYS HAVE FUNNY HAIRCUTS?
2. DO YOU HOT TUB?
3. HOW DO YOU THINK THE BLUE JAYS WILL DO THIS YEAR? THAT BAD, EH?

*Just like today.

CHAPTER FOURTEEN
THEY ALWAYS GET THEIR PERSON!

One of the most recognized Canadian symbols is cherished by millions around the world as a beacon of right, might, and steadfast courage. It has been taken to countries far and wide and shared with friends and strangers as a Canadian cultural icon. Of course, I speak of the hockey puck. But since a chapter on a hard rubber disk could get boring, I will share with you the birth and history of another Canadian institution – The Royal Canadian Mounted Police.

To realize the full impact of this storied law enforcement organization, we must return to the beginning. The first name of the RCMP was actually the North West Mounted Police. Eventually, the name was changed because they realized that the need for police was just as acute in the south and east.

The NWMP was formed by P.M. Sir Johnny Macdonald in 1873, as he wanted to establish a force to bring law and order to the massive swath of land that stretched from Manitoba to the North Pole. He did some quick math and figured that a few guys on horseback should do the trick. He also put them in bright red coats, which many believe was an homage to the British Redcoats. There was, however, a more practical reason. The Americans were having a nasty war with the First Nations south of the border, and he didn't want his troopers getting shot by Natives mistaking them for Yankees, or even Mets. It's similar to the practice of American travellers sewing the Maple Leaf on their backpacks when visiting foreign places like Germany and Moncton.

So why did Johnny Mac bring this force into being in the first place? Well, there were Americans bringing booze across the border into the West, just like today. One of the most notorious locations for this illegal activity was the aptly-named "Fort Whoop-Up". It was located in present-day Alberta, which is just outside of Saskatchewan. The fort was in a strategic location, meaning that the traders could sneak the illegal whisky across from the U.S. and get back home before the cops showed up. In any event, Sir John wanted to shut down this heinous trade so that his government could get the monopoly on it.

Getting men to sign up for an adventure of this type sounds like an easy task, but even though most of the officers were illiterate, they took a look around and realized that there were no women present. The lack of women was a real problem for the younger recruits, but for the older, married officers the journey west was seen as an opportunity to "get away from it all", so to speak.

The trek westward from Manitoba to Alberta was to take a few weeks at most, but many difficulties kept the NWMP from keeping to this tight schedule. On the first day, the new recruits jumped on their horses, and with bugles blaring, red coats gleaming, and swords waving, they charged towards their inevitable victory! That night, they sat around their fires listening to their growling stomachs. It is important to note that the food carts were being pulled by oxen whose maximum speed is similar to that of a Canada Post delivery truck. Once the food caught up, and the men had their fill of food, sleep, and poison ivy, they resumed their journey of destiny, but a bit more slowly this time. One must remember that there were no roads, and the maps they used were very rudimentary.* But they slogged on across treacherous terrain, over rushing rivers, and through clouds of mosquitoes.

They even made a detour to find a guide who could give them directions, something this historian's father would never do. Soon,** they came to Fort Whoop-Up. They got their guide to scout the area out to make sure no one would ambush them this close to victory in their noble quest.

ANOTHER CLASSIC CANADIAN CONVERSATION!

OFFICER: Go scout the area so we don't get ambushed.

GUIDE: I dunno. Looks pretty quiet to me.

OFFICER: I hear there might be women there.

GUIDE: (running towards the fort) Hello! Any ambushes here?

Unfortunately for the guide and the other men, there were no women at the fort, but there were also no ambushes. The Americans had already fled back to the States and didn't return. The NWMP had travelled so far, for so long, that they were pretty ticked at coming up empty-handed, so they began an aggressive search through the entire region for illegal whisky trading. They did find a number of operations, and when they did, they destroyed everything of value and dumped the whisky in the river. Yes, many settlers were sober that winter, and any fish the locals caught nearby didn't have the same fight in them as in previous years. It should be noted that they (the fish) had slightly "distilled" taste when eaten.

*Rudimentary: An old Cree word meaning "White man gets lost again".
**Twelve years later

The NWMP continued their heroic campaign against those who would hamper the government's efforts to settle that vast expanse of space. Out of these stories, many legends were born, the most famous being that of Sam "Woody" Steele. Sgt. Steele was in the NWMP for most of the glory days (Mondays and Wednesdays) and earned quite a reputation for heroism despite being sober. During the Klondike Gold Rush (see Chapter Sixteen) Steele constantly kept the peace between drunk miners and other drunk miners. Once an American miner drew a pistol on Steele, threatening to kill him, but Steele answered him calmly, saying, "I think it's time you went back to the States, and if you are gone by sundown, I won't arrest you, eh?" For his relentless pursuit of peace and justice, he was dubbed the "Lion of the Yukon", which really made him stand out even more, considering how few lions there are in the Yukon. Shortly after this, he fought in the Boer War where he earned the moniker "Polar Bear of Africa".

In 1920, the Canadian government found itself rather bored, so, in typical government fashion, it looked to fix something that wasn't broken. It quickly found an answer in the NWMP. A spokesperson was quoted as saying, "If we change the name to something else, I dunno, maybe...'Crazy Canuck Trooper Squad', we can spend millions on creating new uniforms, flags, crests, and hats. We'll even have to print out new letterheads and envelopes, and all sorts of stationery to replace the old stuff. On an unrelated note, I have a cousin who runs a printing press..."

So, the name change was made, but a more noble name was settled upon, which was, of course, the Royal Canadian

COFFEE BREAK AT RCMP

Mountie Police. Their stories fueled a new genre of movie stars and Hollywood bestowed a well-known motto on the force: "They always get their guy".

STUDY QUESTIONS

1. CAN YOU THINK OF A BETTER NAME FOR A WHISKY TRADING POST THAN "FORT WHOOP-UP"?

2. NEITHER CAN WE.

3. DO YOU PREFER RCMP OR "CRAZY CANUCK TROOPER SQUAD"? EXPLAIN.

CHAPTER FIFTEEN
A RIELLY SERIOUS TIME

If you've been paying attention during the reading of this book,* then you'll notice how often there were actual violent events in our nation's history. We Canucks tend to pride ourselves on our ability to get things done without resorting to violent means, but now you know the truth, sort of.

Anyways, we're going to head back a few pages and dig up the name of Louis Riel. Remember him? He's the guy who tried to set up a proper, effective government in Manitoba and failed, much like every politician since. Guess what? He's back, baby!

That's right! Riel returned to Manitoba in 1885 after spending time in the U.S. trying to get support to throw off the shackles of the Canadian government in Manitoba and replace it with the shackles of the American government. Since he had no success, his return to Canada was a last-ditch effort to become the first Métis provincial leader, but things didn't quite turn out the way he hoped.

Many people flocked to Riel believing that since he came from the States, he must be the answer to their prayers!** They grabbed their guns and began fighting against the North West

*Congratulations.
**How things have changed, eh?

Mounted Police for control of the territory. The two forces couldn't be more different. The Métis were a rag-tag band of men who had few modern weapons, while the government force of militia and Mounties were well-fed, well-armed, and wore bright red uniforms that earned them the nickname "The Santas of the Prairies". While the Métis were happy to crawl around in the dirt and muck in order to win the day, the strict cleaning regimen of the government troops demanded that their uniforms remained dirt-free.

The Métis did quite well at first and won a number of early skirmishes. Their main tactic was to throw handfuls of dirt at their foe, causing the red-clad soldiers to stop what they were doing and tend to their laundry. Many a trooper ended up with badly pruned fingers. Sadly, like the Leafs, a good start means nothing if you can't win at home, and the superior firepower of the government pushed the Métis back.

The final battle happened on May 9, 1885 at Batoche, somewhere in Saskatchewan. The Métis were so hard-pressed that they had run out of bullets for their guns, and were forced to shoot rocks, nails, marshmallows – anything they could get their hands on. They were even out of dirt by this point, so the troopers red coats remained clean. Soon, the Métis ran out of rocks, and their houses all fell over because of the lack of nails. S'mores were a distant memory. Riel tried to run to the States, but they heard he was coming and closed the country. Ol' Louis had no choice but to surrender.

Sir John A. Macdonald had a tough choice ahead: hang Riel for treason, or shoot Riel for treason? He really didn't want to make a martyr out of Riel, but he didn't want a third uprising out West.

RIEL RUNS OUT OF LUCK

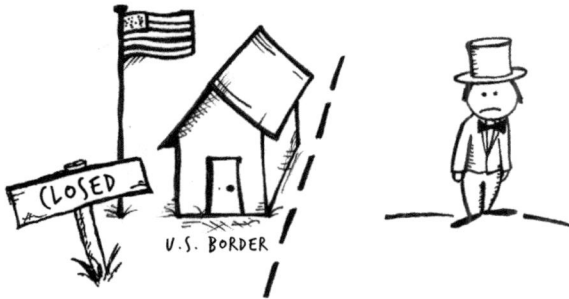

U.S. BORDER

A new thought then came to him – to have Riel declared crazy, and therefore innocent of all the stuff he did. Although this tactic has gained much traction since, Riel did not want to be declared crazy, even though his refusal meant certain death.

Riel is a polarizing figure in Canadian historical debates, and while some declare him a crazy person, others say he was totally bonkers. A third group claims that he would have won more battles if he hadn't run out of nails and dirt. Love him or hate him, Riel is an important figure in Canadian history, and the definite proof of this is that there are two chapters dedicated to him in this book.

STUDY QUESTIONS

1. DO YOU DO YOUR OWN LAUNDRY?
2. HAVE YOU EVER HAD A HANDFUL OF DIRT THROWN AT YOU?
3. WAS THE PERSON WHO THREW IT BONKERS?

CHAPTER SIXTEEN
THERE'S GOLD IN THOSE RIVERS, EH!

"GOLD!" Never has any single word caused so many people to stop whatever they were doing and begin acting like total morons.

In 1898 (or so) gold was discovered in small quantities in an area called the Klondike, just north of Vancouver, and to the right of Alaska. Word quickly spread around the area* and soon men flocked north like geese in the winter. Or is it summer? Whichever it is, they flocked like crazy to find their fortunes in the rivers of the Klondike. Sadly, unless their fortunes were frostbitten toes, most were bound to be disappointed. And, unlike other gold rushes, the

BOB'S "HONEST" SCALES

AMOUNT OF GOLD
PROSPECTORS EXPECTED
TO FIND

ACTUAL
AMOUNT OF
GOLD FOUND

*The entire planet

NWMP (of Chapter Thirteen fame) set some very strict rules for would-be gold hunters. Most of the gold was in such a remote area that people had to take either a boat or plane to get there. Since planes hadn't been invented yet, boats were the mode of choice. And, at each place where a boat would begin or end a leg of the journey, the NWMP would set up a checkpoint to make sure each person had enough supplies to last the harsh winter. The list of required items included: 200 pounds of bacon (do we *really* need to go on?), 400 pounds of flour, and 100 pounds of sugar. It is obvious to this historian that kosher vegan diabetics wouldn't have fared too well in the Klondike gold rush.

♛MEANWHILE, IN AMERICA...

News of the Canadian gold rush reached the States, and thousands of men piled into boats, hoping to strike it rich. Unfortunately, many of them didn't have sufficient supplies, as seen by the American list of requirements:

1. *Two pistols, 1000 rounds of ammunition for each.*
2. *A ham sandwich. (Optional)*

Despite the massive amounts of supplies needed, tens of thousands of treasure seekers made the treacherous journey over the mountains and down the rivers to the Yukon. Upon arrival, they found that a small city had sprung up virtually overnight. It was every bit as cosmopolitan and modern as any other city – like Moose Jaw, for instance.

With so many men arriving in such a short time in such a small place, vice became a lucrative business. Shopkeepers began to dabble in more than just tools. You can see for yourself in the following...

🗨CLASSIC CANADIAN CONVERSATION!

MINER: Where'dya keep yer shovels?

STOREKEEPER: Just past the roulette wheel.

MINER: O'er by them whisky barrels?

STOREKEEPER: Yes, just to the left of the redhead.

MINER: Oh,...uh...what'd I come in here fer?

Many miners ended up with nothing to their name but a broken shovel and a healthy dose of the Clap.

Some folks did actually make some money panning for gold in the Klondike. Unfortunately, few of them made enough to even pay for their supplies, and those who made a fortune rarely spent it wisely, just like lottery winners today.

🗨ANOTHER CLASSIC CANADIAN CONVERSATION!

MINER 1: I made a hunnert thousand bucks in gold!

MINER 2: Good for you! Wanna buy a bridge?

MINER 1: Cool! (Hands over money)

MINER 2: Here's the deed. (Hands over a rock)

MINER 1: Hey! This is a rock!

MINER 2: Straight from the river your bridge is on!

MINER 1: Cool!

MINER 3 WITH GUN: BANG! BANG! (Takes money and rock)

Still others would take their newfound wealth and invest in other mining opportunities, only to learn that there really isn't much gold in the cow pastures around Saskatoon.

In conclusion, many thousands of people spent all of their money believing that they would get rich overnight, but most just got poor overnight. Before we pass judgement on these folks, we should pause to remember our own financial follies. Time-shares, pyramid schemes, and "Gotta Win Someday" in the fourth race are all examples of things we shouldn't have wasted our time and money on. But at least we aren't squatting in a river freezing our toes off.

That's progress, right?

STUDY QUESTIONS

1. HOW LONG WOULD IT TAKE YOU TO EAT 200 POUNDS OF BACON?
2. HAVE YOU EVER FOUND GOLD?
3. WANNA BUY A BRIDGE?

CHAPTER SEVENTEEN
CANADA'S CENTURY!
(IF THAT'S OKAY WITH EVERYONE, EH?)

At the dawn of the 20th century, the Prime Minister of Canada was Sir Wilfred "I'm on the $5 bill" Laurier. He was the first French-Canadian prime minister, and he uttered a famous phrase that actually seemed a bit 'un-Canadian': "The 20th century belongs to Canada, eh?" Such an arrogant boast would have ticked off the rest of the world, but fortunately, nobody was listening to Canada's leader, much like today.

Laurier's biggest contribution to Canada was his aggressive immigration policy. He saw the bajillion square miles of land out west that wasn't being used by anyone, now that the Natives were safely ensconced on their reserves. But where should he get the immigrants from? Who could fill the land, work the soil, and shovel the snow?

His ad campaign was aimed at Europe and had to appeal to the individual regions. Here are a few examples of his slogans:

To Russia: Warmer than Siberia!
To Poland: Far from Russia!
To Ireland: Leprechaun free since 1882!

To Germany: Our sausage isn't the wurst!

To Italy: You'll pasta test!

To Ukraine: Ukraine's loss is your grain!

To Sweden: You'll feel Bjorn anew!

Laurier tried many tactics to get these hearty* folk to immigrate (or is it emigrate?), but the singularly most effective tool at his disposal was the ability to give each family free land.

That's right, each new family would receive 160 acres (2.4 decalitres) of free land! But it was also expected that they would clear the land and start growing food. The good news was that free land would never be available in Europe; the bad news was

*Hearty: Old Latin word meaning "None too bright, but good with a shovel".

POPULATION COMPARISON - 1900

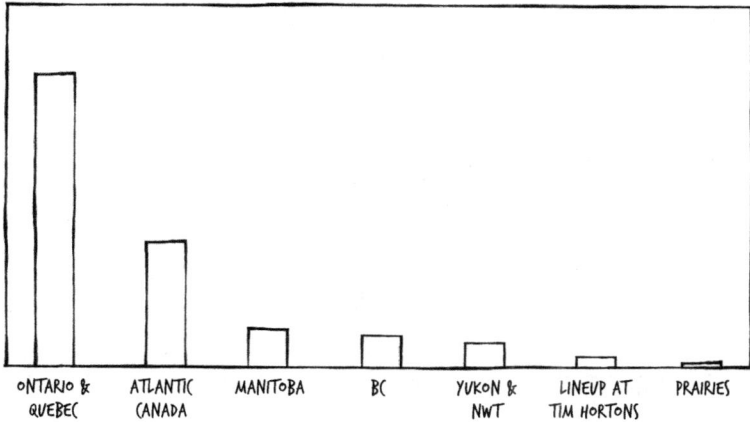

ONTARIO & QUEBEC | ATLANTIC CANADA | MANITOBA | BC | YUKON & NWT | LINEUP AT TIM HORTONS | PRAIRIES

that these folks, hard working as they were, didn't bring any tools with them. You see, most of them had been working as tenant farmers, so they didn't own the land, tools, animals or even their own houses. So, when they left, they couldn't bring anything with them unless they smuggled it in, much like Canadians today coming home after 'visiting friends' in the States. Government inspectors travelled around to ensure that the land was being put to good use, and if not, the settlers would be escorted back to the boat.

Although most settlers were able to afford new tools in order to start farming in the first couple of years, some ran into that pesky truth that they had no tools to do the job properly, and couldn't afford new ones because the land hadn't made them any money yet. (This is similar to job hunting – you can't get a job without experience, but can't get experience without a job. It's nice to know you weren't the first to go through it, eh?)

💬ANOTHER CLASSIC CANADIAN CONVERSATION!

GOV'T INSPECTOR: So, how's the settling coming along?

IMMIGRANT: Oh, it's pretty tough.

GOV'T INSPECTOR: How's that?

IMMIGRANT: We got no tools.

GOV'T INSPECTOR: Well, what did you use in Europe?

IMMIGRANT: Boss's tools, but we couldn't bring them with us.

GOV'T INSPECTOR: Ah. Well, better get that field plowed by next week, or you'll lose the land, eh?

IMMIGRANT: But I got no plow, or even a horse to pull it.

GOV'T INSPECTOR: Sounds good. Welcome to Canada, eh!

Word got back to the government that many new immigrants had no means to clear and develop the land. Once again, our government sprang into action! They formed a 200-man committee to figure out how to approach this problem in such a way as to get themselves re-elected. This committee shrewdly decided to give out free tools to those who needed them so they could make the land productive. The fact that it plunged the government into debt paled in comparison to ensuring a win in the next election. Makes you proud to be Canadian, eh?

🏆MEANWHILE, IN AMERICA...

The American West was being settled as well, and some famous stories were being born, the most famous being "The Shoot-out at the O.K. Corral" (starring Kurt Russell and Val Kilmer). There were countless similar tales that weren't quite as famous, but they did uphold the tradition of focussing on the "shooting" and not the "corralling".

WHY EUROPEANS CAME TO CANADA — 1900–1930

ICE AND SNOW

KILTS

LUTEFISK

ICE AND SNOW

ICE AND SNOW

LEPRECHAUNS

CRUMPETS

WHALES

BIG MOUSTACHES

GOATS

CZARS

WEIRD CHEESE

HEIDI

FUNNY CLOTHES

BANDITS

WHINE

BULLS

RUINS

MORE RUINS

TURKEYS

The West opened up to a million settlers, many from Europe, who were drawn there by the promise of free land and week-long blizzards. With all of these new people coming to Canada, the stage had been set for a new era of hope. Hope for the future. Yes, an era of brotherhood, prosperity, and peace for all. And that era was called: The First World War.

STUDY QUESTIONS

1. HAVE YOU SEEN LAURIER ON THE $5 BILL?
2. DID YOU KNOW THAT HE LOOKS LIKE MR. SPOCK FROM STAR TREK?
3. GOOGLE IT.

CHAPTER EIGHTEEN
TROUBLE IN THE OLD COUNTRY

In the early 20th century, times were good. Canada was becoming populated with many newcomers, and the West was teeming with people. The population density skyrocketed to 0.0002 people per square mile, a higher ratio than sober fans at a Nickelback concert. But these "salad days" of Canada weren't to last. Murmurs in Europe soon turned to rumblings, and then skipped right over grumblings and went straight to shootings. Here is a quick, easy, step-by-step account of the causes of World War I:

Step 1: Man shoots two people riding in their car.

Step 2: Relatives of the shot people start shooting relatives of the shooter.

Step 3: Friends of newly-shot relatives vow to protect surviving members of original shooter's family.

Step 4: Friends of relatives of the originally-shot people vow to shoot the original shooter's family and friends.

Step 5: More friends of the original shooter's friends vow to make the friends of the shot relatives pay for shooting at their friends.

Step 6:   Still more friends join with the Step 5 friends in vowing to make the original shooter's friends safe from the originally-shot people's friends and their friends.

Step 7:   Some guys who aren't really tight with either the shooter and his friends or the shoot-ees and their friends (but who like to play with guns) join up with the shot people's relatives and friends and begin to shoot at the friends of original shooter's family's friends of friends and their friends.

Actually, as we look at the above steps, it can be clearly seen that World War One could have been an episode of The *A-Team*, but with real bullets.

Thankfully, we had moved from Laurier and on to Robert "I'm on the $100 bill" Borden. He was a no-nonsense leader and decided to approach the war from a decidedly Canadian point of view: what does Britain want us to do? (Today, it's: "What does America want us to do? Let's do the opposite.") Well, Britain asked very politely if all of their nice little colonial children wouldn't mind too much lending them a hand, and Canada fell into line quickly, pledging half a million troops. The pledging was easy – it was making good on the promise that was the tough part. But Canadian lads rushed to sign up and fight for Mother England. Winter was fast approaching, which made the option of getting shot at in Belgium seem like a better time than shovelling snow in 30-below weather.

As World War I got going, Our Side, known as the Triple Entente* consisted of four empires: Britain (and all her colonies),

*Which means "Three Empires"

France, Italy, and Russia. The Central Powers (The Other Guys) were made up of Germany (Huns), Austria-Hungary, and also Turkey, who felt like playing war because it had been a while. Bulgaria had also joined the Central Powers, but they missed rehearsal and decided to just stay home and drink – a custom that remains to this day.

Like so many wars, in so many places, the troops left for the battlefields with the promise of returning by Kwanzaa. Unfortunately, they didn't specify which year that would be, so people were disappointed for a while. Many recent arrivals to Canada returned to fight in the conflict. Some came from Germany, and if they could make it back to their homeland, they would be fighting against Canadians. Still others were too old to fight, and instead of heading back to Germany, they would try to blend in to Canadian society. Anti-German sentiment was running high, so they had to be careful.

💬 A CLASSIC CANADIAN CONVERSATION!

BRITISH IMMIGRANT: I say, the lads should give those Huns a good wallop, wot!

GERMAN IMMIGRANT: Ja.

BRITISH IMMIGRANT: (suspiciously) What was that?

GERMAN IMMIGRANT: I am meaning, gut riddance to zee Hun, und all zat!

BRITISH IMMIGRANT: Bloody right!

GERMAN IMMIGRANT: Ja.

The rallying cry for Canadian troops was "Come Fight for Mother England!", (which narrowly beat out "Come Die in

Europe!") and tens of thousands answered the call, mainly because they were so ticked at being unemployed for so long they wanted to shoot somebody. Unfortunately, the rifles they were supplied with weren't quite up to the standards of muddy warfare. The Ross Rifle, designed by Mr. R. Rifle, was a very effective gun when out on a Sunday stroll through moose-infested woods, but the slightest bit of mud would make it jam up. When casualties mounted because their guns kept failing, the Army issued a helpful decree: "Keep your rifles clean and you might not die."

WORLD WAR I (A HANDY MAP)

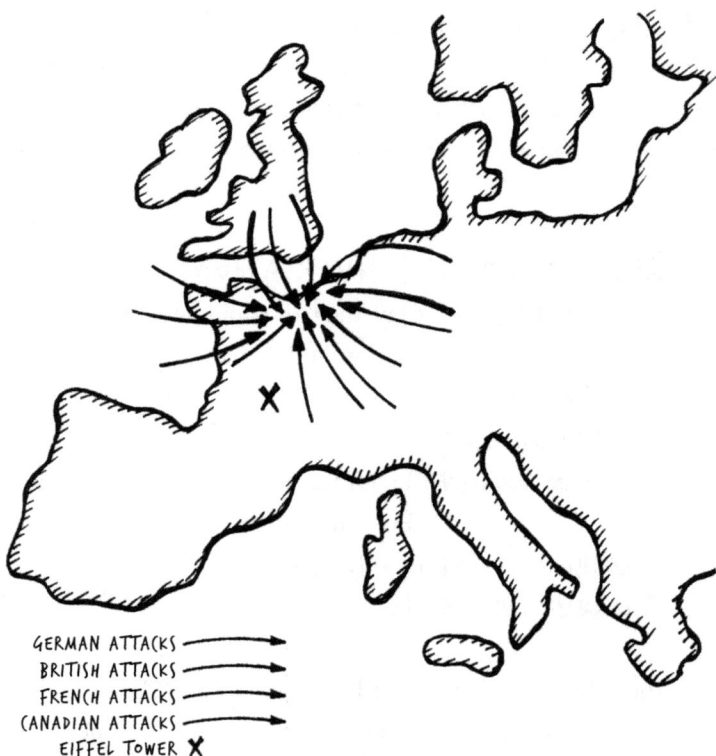

GERMAN ATTACKS ⟶
BRITISH ATTACKS ⟶
FRENCH ATTACKS ⟶
CANADIAN ATTACKS ⟶
EIFFEL TOWER ✗

Unlike previous conflicts where armies would line up and charge each other until one side decided to see how fast they could run away, this war bogged down in the mud. The difference came about one day when some guy said, "I say, if we dig holes and get in them, the bullets will fly right over us, wot! Brilliant!" So, the shovels went to work and before long the trenches stretched for hundreds of miles from the English Channel to Scotland. Then that same guy said, "These trenches would be much more useful on the other side, you know, where the war is, wot!" So, they dug trenches that stretched for hundreds of miles on the other side, only to find out that the Germans had done it, too. The Brits were so upset that the Huns had taken their idea that they ordered their men to leave the cover of the trenches and go tell the Germans how nasty they were for copying their idea. After the first million casualties, the British figured that the Germans had gotten the message and waited for a better idea.

A better idea came in the form of Team A sending a bajillion artillery shells screaming over to Team B's trenches. Then, Team A could leave the trenches and stroll across the muddy land and simply take the trenches from Team B because they had to be dead, or at the very least, quite uncomfortable. But some Team A players were very polite about the whole war thing, so they wouldn't attack until Team B was ready.

After a five-hour artillery bombardment:

British: I say, Mr. Hun, we are coming over, wot! Are you ready?

German: Ah, if you could please give us chance to get zee

schnitzels cooked und machine guns set up, zat
vould help, ja.

British: Fine. We'll be over in, say, ten minutes? We'll whistle
before we come.

German: Zat is most kind.

British: Not at all.

Naturally, by the time Team A arrived, Team B was ready to
fight, and Team A would have to retreat back to their trenches
and wait for Team B's artillery to scream down on them. And this
process repeated itself every day for three years.

Sometime during this craziness, a group of generals on Our
Side got together to celebrate the latest failed charge when a few
of the smarter ones offered a bright idea: *leave the trenches while
we are still bombing Team B. Then, we'll get to their trenches and
surprise them before they're ready! Oh, and don't whistle first.* This
group included a Canadian general named Arthur Currie, and by
using this neato strategy, the Canadians took Vimy Ridge, a most
unpleasant place that the Germans had held for three years. After
suffering over a bajillion dead and wounded British and French
troops, people thought that it would be impossible to take the
Ridge, but the Canadian brass had yet another bright idea. They
told the troops that if they won the battle they could stay in France.
If they lost, they had to go back to Canada and shovel snow. They
took the ridge in three hours, resulting in many Germans running
away, cold schnitzels left behind.

There were many examples of Canadian heroism, and even
the Germans knew things would be bad when they found out
Canadians were facing them. The British Prime Minister, Lloyd

"Call me Larry" George stated, "Whenever the Germans found the Canadian Corps coming into the line they prepared for the worst!" A German officer was also quoted as saying, "Canadians? Das ist nein gut! Vee should gettin' zee gone!" We were so effective as an army that the Germans began to say we must be cheating, but we couldn't hear them through the clouds of poison gas they sent our way.

Yes, we won WWI, and things were terrible in Europe, but Canada had its own struggles on the home front. Fewer and fewer willing recruits were left in Canada, and seeing the wounded come home didn't encourage them to sign up. English Canada had sent plenty, but French Canada didn't get all misty-eyed about France's predicament. Remember Chapter Six? They did. Now they called France "A few acres of mud", and when the army recruiters came by they just snickered and went back to their poutine.

One important Canadian institution saw its birth during the war: income tax. Borden's government had to get some money to pay for all of the malfunctioning Ross rifles, and those kickbacks didn't look after themselves. Of course, it promised to get rid of the tax once the war was over, but we all know how that turned out. When the people voted Borden's government out of power because it refused to do-away with the tax, people pressured the new government (King's) to follow through. King responded by saying that he wasn't the one that brought it in, so he wasn't responsible for it. (It must be noted that the new government did issue free pencils to all Canadians to so they could get their returns done*.) WWI was simply bad.

In WWI, billions died, although I may have added wrong. Suffice to say it was nicknamed "The War to End All Wars for 21

---

*The pencils were paid for with taxes, of course.

Years". On November 11, 1918, at 11 o'clock in the morning, at the eleventh minute, and the eleventh second, the treaty of peace was signed. It was a miraculous feat, having so many people sign in one second, but it happened and peace would reign. This solemn day is remembered each year in Canada as a Statutory Holiday.

STUDY QUESTIONS

1. HAVE YOU BEEN TO A NICKELBACK CONCERT? WHY?
2. WHO DO YOU THINK NAMED TURKEY?
3. ISN'T COLD SCHNITZEL TERRIBLE? EXPLAIN.

CHAPTER NINETEEN
THE GOOD, THE BAD, AND THE CRAZY

After the war, Canada continued to be a pretty good place to be, unless you lived in Winnipeg.* No, it wasn't because of the weather, the mosquitoes, or the return of Louis Riel; it was because of the Winnipeg General Strike of 1919.

Winnipeg was the largest Canadian city west of Toronto and was the proud owner of almost a hundred labour unions. All of those unions decided to strike because the factory owners and bosses had made a ton of money on the war by having the wives of soldiers work, but wouldn't share the profits with the workers, just like today. When the husbands returned, the wives went back home and the men went to work.

Picture this: the men, who have just gone through horrific times in the trenches, returned to work and felt they had to strike because conditions weren't very good. Things must have been pretty bad if the workplace was a step down from the trenches. The strikers demanded better pay, better working conditions, and a cream-cheese bagel every Monday. Management counter-offered with bagels every-other Monday, and the strike was on!

The police were quite worried, since there were over 30,000 strikers in the streets, but they soon relaxed because, in typically

*Winnipeggers, don't get mad. I lived there for a couple of years, so I understand.

Canadian style, the strikers brought no guns. The police, along with the strike-breakers, crashed into the mob and when the dust settled, two people were dead and a couple dozen were wounded. It was a shock to Winnipeg, as this was the largest confrontation the city had seen since the Great Winnipeg Pie Fight of 1909.*

The decade from 1920–1929 was known by a few names: The Roaring 20's, The Jazz Hands Age, and The Aspirin Age. The last name was given because hockey players hadn't invented the helmet yet. Times were good, and parties were on every night, in every town and city, as people tried to forget the war. Cities began to grow, and more and more Europeans were flocking to Canada because it was so peaceful, despite the first four paragraphs.

Unfortunately, even during this happy time, there was an elephant in the room: women. Well, not women exactly, but the *rights* of women in Canada, which were pretty non-existent at the time. One must realize that at this time, women in Canada were not considered 'persons'. Sure, they could cook, clean, and make babies, but they were prevented from voting, driving, or owning a personal computer. This was just too much for one particular woman, Emily Murphy. She began an intense campaign to get women recognized as actual people in Canada so they could have the same rights as men. Her battle cry was "All women (except Natives and Asians) deserve the same rights as men!"

Her passion drove the Canadian government to make an important proclamation, and that was, "Hey, Emily! Shut up and make babies!" But Emily was not to be denied, or pregnant, and she got the British Privy Council involved. Tired of answering her emails and phone messages, they finally broke down and said,

*We made this up, but it sounds like fun, eh?

"Fine! You're a person! Now, go make babies and leave us alone!" It was a huge victory for women's rights (except Natives and Asians) and was welcomed by women across the country (except Natives and Asians), who celebrated this historic event by making their husbands an extra-special meal, and then cleaning up afterwards.

NOTE: You should know that Emily had four friends (none were men) who helped her in this noble quest. They were like the all-female Ghostbusters, with less technology but more swagger.

☗ MEANWHILE, IN AMERICA...

Black Tuesday, 1929. People in New York City had been partying so hard that they forgot to pay the electric bill, and the lights went out. Usually, that's not a problem, but the stock exchange was plunged into darkness. With a "the show must go on" attitude, they continued to yell and wave little pieces of paper around, not realizing that they were trading Chinese take-out menus. When the lights came on, everyone was tired and hungry, and also broke, since they had been paying hundreds of dollars for pieces of paper printed, not with shares in valuable companies, but with "Lucky Golden Dragon Chinese Food Restaurant and Laundromat". When the traders realized what had happened, they gave up and went home, some by choosing to fly out of their 12th-storey windows.

Canadians didn't escape unscathed, and many had their savings wiped out. A large number of businesses simply didn't have the money to keep their doors open, and they had to shut down, laying off thousands of workers. It was like a dress rehearsal for the 1980's. Even politicians felt the pinch, and would have to settle for a paltry 60% pay raise that year. The Great Depression was on, and we moved from the Roaring 20's to the Dirty 30's.

N.Y.S.E. SEPTEMBER 29TH, 1929

HELLO? YEAH I'LL HAVE A #6, #8, TWO #12'S AND $1,000 IN GOLD!

To compound the money problem, Mother Nature decided to take some time off, and the Prairies, the "Bread Basket and Bun Bowl of Canada", got no rain. The land dried up, and with it, the fortunes of thousands of farmers. The soil was as dry as *Front Page Challenge* (remember that show?), and with no plants growing, it simply blew away into far-off places, such as Sweden. A small glimmer of hope was represented by the First Annual Canadian Amateur Football Championship, won by the Destitute Farmers who beat the Unemployed Factory Workers 17–14. The trophy was a sack of potatoes.

It was during this dismal time in Canadian history that, in order to cheer people up, the Prime Minister decided to call an election. The P.M. at this time was one Mackenzie "I'll ask Mother" King, the great-great-great grandson of the not-so-great William Lyon Mackenzie from Chapter 9(a). Mackenzie King ruled during the highest unemployment rates that Canada would see until Mulroney (see Chapter Twenty-four, but watch your wallet). King tried a number of tactics to get money moving so Canadians could get back to work, but despite great ideas like the "Parliament Hill Bake Sale and Chili Cook-Off", the cash simply wouldn't flow.

King won the election in a landslide, mainly because his opposition, Arthur "Beat King" Meighan, ran on the platform of "Get to work, you lazy slobs". But King wasn't out of the woods yet. Canada was still mired in the Great Depression, and people looked to their leader for help. But who do leaders look to? Like all good boys, King sought help from his mother. Every day he would seek her advice on matters of national importance, and reminisce about his childhood days. The interesting catch was that his mother had been dead since 1917. Yep, King would talk with his late mother, which may sound crazy, until you realize that he also talked with his dead dogs, so it's all a matter of perspective. The fact that every dog he owned had been named "Pat" is just icing on the cake. (He had one named "Bob", but he thought it was a cat.)

STUDY QUESTIONS

1. DID YOU KNOW WINNIPEG WAS SO EXCITING?

2. IS "THE RETURN OF LOUIS RIEL" A GOOD IDEA FOR A MOVIE? LET ME KNOW.

3. DO YOU PREFER A BAKE SALE OR CHILI COOK-OFF?

CHAPTER TWENTY
DÉJÀ VU ALL OVER AGAIN...

Canada was a pretty peaceful place in the 1930's, mainly because everyone was broke. Most of the stores, factories, restaurants, and arcades were shut down, and a quarter of the work force wasn't working. Even crime dropped because breaking into someone's house held no guarantee of finding something worth swiping. It's been said* that some thieves were so overcome by pity that they actually left money for their would-be victims.

As nice as it was having a peaceful country, Prime Minister Mackenzie King knew that he had to get people working again, even if it meant more break-ins. After talking with Mom and all the Pats, (see last chapter) King still had no ideas that would bail Canada out of this leaky boat. As with many solutions that save a government, this one came from the outside. The helping hand was provided by the generous, kind, and peace-loving folks we now call Nazis.

Apparently, Germany was still pretty sore about losing the last war, and even more sore (sorer?) about the treatment they received at the end of it. So what if they lost an incredibly destructive war that cost millions of lives? That doesn't mean they should be blamed for it, right? Well, the rest of the world did blame Germany, and

*By me

made her pay for it, too. The debt that was heaped on Germany was so stifling that she couldn't get financing for a sauerkraut sandwich. But now, she wanted to get things back to the way they were, and figured the best way out of the predicament she was in because of the last war was to start a whole new war. Their leader, Adolf "I like brown shirts and white people" Hitler convinced most of Germany that he could save her by doing all sorts of creative things like building highways and invading the Soviet Union. But I'm jumping ahead.

When 1938 rolled along, Our Side (the same ones from WWI minus Italy) was woefully unprepared for Hitler's aggressive tantrums at the conferences. He'd fall to the floor and kick and scream until the other delegates would give in and say things like, "Fine! Take the land! Just shut up, already!" Hitler would cheer up and everyone would leave as friends. Hitler would go back to Germany and polish up his tank divisions while the rest would go back home and say things like, "Peace in our time, except for Czechoslovakia!"

Of course, Hitler wasn't happy to stop at his tantrums, and he had a bunch of toys he wanted to try out on exotic locations such as Poland. And so, on September 1, 1939, Germany invaded. In response, Britain quickly declared war on Germany. She expected all her colonial children to do the same, but Canada waited a whole week to do so, just to show we were all growed-up. We still had to ask Britain for the keys to the car, but it was a start.

Once the war got rolling, the Canadian economy began to pick up again. Factories would soon be staffed by the wives of the men who signed up to be soldiers, and neato things like guns, bombs, and portable latrines would make their way to

TECHNOLOGICAL ADVANCES DURING CHAPTER 20

IN CANADA
FREDERICK BANTING
DEVELOPED INSULIN TO
SAVE MILLIONS OF LIVES!

IN GERMANY
ADOLF HITLER
DEVELOPED A WAR MACHINE
TO END MILLIONS OF LIVES!

(SEE WHAT HAPPENS WHEN YOU DON'T EAT ENOUGH POUTINE?)

the front. P.M. King thanked his lucky stars, his dead dogs, and his late mother for coming through for him. Over the radio he told the Canadian people that things were going to get much better, now that the Great Depression was but a happy memory. He trumpeted that he had found a way out for all Canadians, and they should follow his strong, decisive, and charismatic leadership! To be honest, King was concerned about trying to raise an army after the carnage of World War I. He needn't have feared.

💬A CLASSIC CANADIAN CONVERSATION!

MAN 1: You wanna go fight the Germans and maybe die?

MAN 2: Will I have to listen to King's radio speeches anymore?

MAN 1: Nope.

MAN 2: Where do I sign up?

The first couple years of the war were not what one would call "successful", unless one was a Nazi. The Other Guys (Germany, Italy, and Japan) had spent the Dirty 30's building tanks, planes, and massive warships that were bigger than the hometown I grew up in*. Meanwhile, "Our Side" (pretty much the rest of the planet) had spent the last decade doing trivial things like feeding their people, curing yellow fever, and inventing deodorant.

♛MEANWHILE, IN AMERICA...

The U.S. was simply not prepared for war. They got into WWI near the end and figured they'd do the same this time around. There were a lot of immigrants in the U.S., and many wanted to return to their homelands to fight for freedom, but most Americans wanted to sit this one out. That all changed on December 7th, 1941, when Hitler called U.S. President Roosevelt a "pansy". After all, some things are worth fighting for.

As in World War One, Canadians fought bravely in every theatre of war, including the Cineplex in downtown Regina when they ran out of buttery topping. And even though the fighting is highlighted, they also spread many of our national treasures around the globe such as maple syrup, politeness, and dog sledding. The

---

*Elgin, Ontario: Birthplace of the snowdrift, specifically, in our driveway.

latter didn't really catch on in South East Asia, which already had its focus on championship cockroach racing.

Eventually, the war stretched around the world and it was, overall, a nasty bit of business. Except for Antarctica, Canada was the most peaceful place to live during the conflict. Sure, there was rationing of things like meat, butter, and sugar, but in some places they were eating their shoes, so we couldn't really complain.

Thanks to the miracles of technology, there were new and wonderful ways to kill people in World War Two. Gone were the days of walking across the ground, rifle in hand, hoping for a nice trench to hop into. Now the bomber, the aircraft carrier, and the rocket allowed people to stay far away from the conflict while 'greeting' the enemy in a very personal way. Armies could now inflict massive casualties on the other side without disrupting important events such as cricket matches.

Politicians also used this time to leave their mark on the pages of history by making grandiose speeches over the radio waves:

Churchill: "Never has so much been owed by so many to so few – until credit cards get invented."

Stalin: "We have more men than you have bullets, and we're willing to prove it!"

Roosevelt: "Sorry that we're late, again. But we brought nukes!"

King: "Mom says 'Hi'."

Life in Canada was fairly typical during the war, and Mother Nature returned to bring some much-needed rain to the Prairies. Wheat was growing once again, although Canadians couldn't eat it because of the wartime rationing. Many a parent dangled socks full of wheat just above the heads of disobedient children, much like today's parents dangle video game controllers or college tuition cheques.

After the first surge of patriotism saw thousands of Canadian men run off to fight, King did have a spot of trouble raising more troops to sign up. Too many people remembered the First World War and didn't want shiploads of wounded returning home. It looked as though he may have to do the unthinkable: declare *conscription*. Forcing Canadian men to go to war wasn't very "Canadian", but King was able to dodge the bullet by using a phrase that still confuses people and also kept him in power: "Conscription if necessary, but not necessarily conscription, unless it's necessarily necessary."

The war had more ups and downs than a week on the Toronto Stock Exchange, but by the end, it had more ups than downs, unlike the Toronto Stock Exchange. The map of Europe and been redrawn so dramatically that people needed a scorecard to keep track of who owned what. Thanks to the tireless efforts of the Allies, Germany was freed from the evil clutches of the Nazis, and was now in the warm embrace of the Communists. Of course, that was only the eastern part of it, because the western part was in the fold of Our Side. Berlin, the largest city, was in East Germany, which was governed from Moscow. It (Berlin) was now divided into four sections: 1/2 Soviet, 1/6 British, 1/6 French, and 1/6 American. Meanwhile, in Canada, Toronto had been divided into 3/5 Canadian, 1/5 Italian, 1/8 Scottish, 1/32 Polish, and 1/472 Egyptian. It was a very confusing time.

During the war, the Canadian government had one of its

many moments we like to call "boneheaded". The Japanese had just taken Hong Kong, killing or capturing all the Canadian troops defending the city. This caused all Japanese people in Canada to instantly become spies and saboteurs. Therefore, the government grabbed all the Japanese in Vancouver, Victoria, and other coastal areas, and shipped them further inland, "away from Tokyo". If relocating them weren't enough, the government also took all their property, since they wouldn't need it in their new homes, also called "tents". After this relocation, the government began interrogating the Japanese, many of them born in Canada, and shipped off any people who didn't end their answer with "eh?".

In the Pacific, the Americans did most of the heavy lifting, and eventually dropped atomic bombs on Japan until they agreed to make us high-quality cars and electronics at competitive prices.* Yes, the war was over, but another conflict was soon to take its place. Although there weren't a lot of shots fired in this conflict, there were numerous clandestine affairs, not unlike a weekend in Vegas. These moments shaped our world and left an indelible mark on history, which will not soon be forgotten. Taken together as a whole, these events are now known, of course, as Chapter Twenty-One.

STUDY QUESTIONS

1. WAS IT A MISTAKE FOR HITLER TO INVADE THE SOVIET UNION?
2. YES, IT WAS.
3. THAT 'YEN' JOKE WAS PRETTY FUNNY, EH?
BONUS QUESTION: WHY IS A 'CLUTCH' ALWAYS EVIL?
WHY NOT 'GOOD' OR 'INDIFFERENT'?

*You could say we had a 'yen' for high tech stuff.

CHAPTER TWENTY-ONE
SHUT THE DOOR! IT'S THE COLD WAR!
(OR: HERE COMES THE BOOM!)

After World War II, everyone was pretty "warred out", as it were. Two global conflicts inside of 30 years will do that to any planet. Canadians wanted to focus on the good things in life: getting jobs, starting families, and avoiding bombs and bullets. This sort of attitude was pretty much everywhere, and most pursuits had a focus on the "starting families" portion.

Nine months and fifteen minutes after the war ended, one billion children were born, causing the largest diaper shortage in human history. Shortly after this "boom" of "babies", the newly minted fathers realized how terrifying children can be and demanded another war so they had a way to escape. But we'll talk about that later. (The war, not the children.)

Although starting a war sounds like an easy task, the world was in such a confused state* that it was hard to tell who Canadians should 'not-like'. (I'd say 'hate', but we're keeping this book family-friendly.) Old enemies were now our friends, and some friends were now our sworn enemies. It was like junior high on a global scale. Canadians are generally nice, of course, but we do love to 'not-like' people on occasion, even in our own borders. Don't believe me?

*Alabama

Maybe you should read a few key chapters of this book again.

Fortunately, a Canadian stepped up in 1948 and told us how things should work between people from now on. John "Nice Guy" Humphrey drafted a very important declaration while working at the United Nations. He wrote this declaration while serving as the Director of Human Rights, and titled it "The Declaration of Human Rights". (Cough.) This mandate stated, in firm, yet poetic tones, that *all* people on Earth, regardless of race, religion, or facial hair, had the absolute right to be *human*. This was widely applauded by (almost) all nations, a notable exception being the Soviet Union, who couldn't clap because their hands were full of guns. This document has been the measuring rod for the U.N. whenever it has to label a certain country or group that seems to be 'not nice'. For instance, in the 1970's, Idi Amin's Uganda was at the level of 'very mean', while Pol Pot's Cambodia was deemed 'downright nasty'. This rating caused them to receive crippling sanctions and lose their membership in the "little countries with nothing the West wants so we'll ignore them" club.

In 1949, Canada's borders were finally where we now recognize them as Newfoundland decided to join up. It is important to note that Newfoundland didn't simply sign on. The citizens actually had three choices: remain a British colony, join Confederation, or go it alone and probably get swallowed up by the Americans. So many choices, so much fishing. What would the good people of that fair region do? The leader at the time was one Joey Smallwood.

Smallwood wanted Newfoundland to join Canada, but many others wanted to remain a British colony. Still others saw America as the horse to bet on. Still others wanted to drink Screech and kiss fish. The situation was confusing for many, but fortunately, we have this first-hand account to fall back on:

💬ANOTHER CLASSIC CANADIAN CONVERSATION!

SEAMUS: Sure bye, dat Joey, he's some nesh. Put us in a clobber, bye.

JIMMY: Dat angishore's got more lip dan a coal bucket, bye.

SEAMUS: But dem Yanks, dey'd have us by de ferks, bye. Ballyrag us good, bye.

JIMMY: Yep. Tom Long's account, bye. I be huffed. Marry up wit Canada, den?

SEAMUS: Dat's de lowest of de fulish, bye.

JIMMY: It's not arse backwards, bye.

SEAMUS: Dwai comin'. Best snug up de frape, bye.

JIMMY: Bye, bye.

As you can plainly see, joining Canada was the wisest choice for Newfoundland, and on March 31, 1949, Canada had ten provinces. Smallwood wanted to sign the document quickly, and did so just before midnight so that Newfoundland wouldn't have its provincial holiday tied to April Fool's Day, thereby avoiding the chance of Newfoundland becoming the target of many jokes for all eternity.

As promised, let's go back to the war the men were asking for. The Korean War was hardly a World War, but it was good enough for thousands of Canadian men to sign up and cross the Pacific, if just to avoid 2:00 a.m. feedings.

The Korean War began in 1950 and lasted for eleven seasons of M*A*S*H. As far as wars go, this one was pretty small, and, if television can be trusted, a lot more fun than the trenches of World War One or the nuclear explosions of World War Two. But the war wasn't to last, and a ceasefire was declared, resulting in Korea being divided *exactly* how it was before a million people died. With the end of the war, the men returned home. Thankfully, the children were too old for the mid-sleep feedings, so the men were happy to come back.

NOT MUCH CHANGED IN CANADA BECAUSE OF THE WAR

"WE LOVE ALL COUNTRIES EXCEPT GERMANY, JAPAN, AND ITALY"

"WE LOVE ALL COUNTRIES EXCEPT THE SOVIET UNION!" (AND MAYBE FRANCE, A LITTLE BIT)

CANADIANS DURING WWII

CANADIANS AFTER WWII

After the Korean Conflict, life in Canada returned to normal: dads went to work, moms stayed home, and kids skipped school. Now that things had gained some measure of stability, Canadians could get on with doing neato things like inventing the Avro Arrow. (This paragraph is purely meant as foreshadowing. My editor says I need to employ more 'high-brow' writing skills so my target audience, and therefore, royalties, will increase. Whatever.) A lot of people scoff at Canada's current military state, and although our men and women in uniform are utmost professionals, a lot of the equipment they have is less effective than what the Métis had in Chapter Fifteen. Their helicopters crash, their submarines spring leaks, and the wi-fi in tanks hardly works at all. When did the government abandon its armed forces to this sorry state of affairs? In short, the answer is 1959.

After World War II, Canada had the third largest navy and fourth largest air force on the planet. It also had proven to the world that its troops were incredibly effective when called upon, and many times Canadian troops were asked to attack where other countries had failed. There was a strong sense of pride and accomplishment that one company hoped to cash in on: A. V. Roe Aircraft Research and Test Crashing Company, otherwise known as Bombardier.*

The company (we'll call it Avro to avoid confusion) built the famous Avro Arrow, a twin-engine fighter that could climb higher, fly further, and lose money faster than any other aircraft in history. It was such a successful aircraft that it almost landed once. Granted, the plane would have more troubles than victories, and the costs soared higher than Icarus defying his father Daedalus's instructions. (I can hear my royalties rolling in...)

As with many projects the Canadian government puts money into, the Arrow went a bajillion dollars over budget, causing the government to take a serious look at throwing more money at it. And throw, they did. Eventually, though, an election year arrived and the government wanted to look like it came to its senses, sort of. The airplane was scrapped, and the money was put into other

*Although it's spelled "Bombardier" it's pronounced "Avro".

COST OF AVRO ARROW

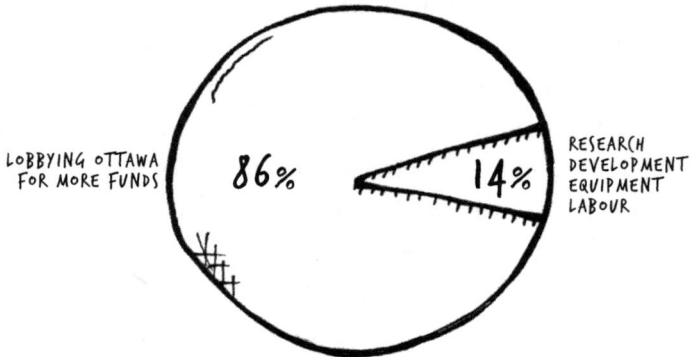

LOBBYING OTTAWA
FOR MORE FUNDS

86%

14%

RESEARCH
DEVELOPMENT
EQUIPMENT
LABOUR

neato projects, like building the Diefenbunker. It only cost half a bajillion dollars, and would protect up to 500 Canadian politicians when the Russians tried to nuke America and missed. Not really a good trade, if you ask me.

When the order came down to cease the Arrow project, it included instructions to chop up the remaining five aircraft and to destroy the blueprints. Although this was verified to have been completed, there are a number of crazy, tinfoil hat-wearing conspiracy nuts who claim they heard one Arrow taking off that morning in the pre-dawn darkness. It's obvious to this historian that what they actually heard was a UFO from Mars.

One of the greatest losses attached to the Arrow fiasco was the loss of brains, and I'm not talking about the government, for once. Thousands of highly skilled engineers were instantly out of work, and since there wasn't a war on, the men had nowhere to go. So, instead of sitting around waiting for the rotary phone to ring, they packed up their lives and headed down to the U.S. and became NASA. Sorry America, it's true. Many of the great

"American" brains that took your astronauts to the moon were raised on poutine and moose meat. This was the first episode in the oft-recurring drama called "brain drain". It's a Canadian tradition to raise and train brilliant scientists, entertainers, and athletes, then send them down to the U.S. in exchange for Jerry Bruckheimer movies. In my opinion, we're getting the short end of the CGI stick.

So, Canada had lost any hope of developing its own military hardware, and it had to buy equipment from other countries, namely, the U.S. of A. They gladly sold us equipment for years, usually after they were done with it.

♔ MEANWHILE, IN AMERICA...

The U.S. military found out which of its tanks, planes, and ships performed poorly in the Korean War and promptly sold them to Canada at crazy-high prices. An American general was quoted as saying, "We're not convinced that humans should actually come in contact with these machines. So, here ya' go, Canada."

This is a tradition that has continued to this very day.

STUDY QUESTIONS

1. HAVE YOU EVER BEEN TO NEWFOUNDLAND? DID YOU MEET THE GUY WHO WENT ICE FISHING AND CAUGHT 20 POUNDS OF ICE?
2. DID YOU "SNUG UP YOUR FRAPE"?
3. SHOULD ICARUS HAVE HEEDED HIS FATHER'S WARNING? EXPLAIN.

CHAPTER TWENTY-TWO
THE COLD WAR CONTINUES...

The Cold War was the first of its kind, and can best be described as a 'First Date'. Both sides were excited that it was happening, and each was looking for success, but that would mean something different to each of them. The Girl might want The Guy to be funny, yet responsible, and she might even want him to hold the car door open for her. The Guy may actually do this, unless his mind is too focused on making sure he's got nothing in his teeth, and he's checking his reflection in the window as inconspicuously as possible. Then The Girl gets tired of waiting and opens it herself, only to smash The Guy's nose with the door frame. (We may or may not be speaking from experience.) Now, where was I? Oh yes, the Cold War meant different things to different people, and first dates suck.

Some good things happened in Canada early on in the Cold war, although we just about dropped the puck on a biggie. A Soviet spy grabbed a bunch of his bosses' secret files and ran to the Canadian Embassy in Ottawa, pleading for his family's safety. That man was Igor "Glasnost" Gouzenko. He was told he was being transferred to sunny Siberia, so he decided to turn against his masters and run into the welcoming arms of Canada. Upon hearing the news of this extremely important defection, Prime

Minister King sprang into action. His mother was strangely silent on the issue, but Pat #3 said "Ruff! Ruff!" which King took for "Send him back to the Russians!" Fortunately, cooler heads prevailed and Gouzenko stayed in Canada, albeit with a pillowcase over his head.

Thanks to Igor's information, we found out that both Canada and the U.S. were riddled with Soviet spies. Canada was embarrassed by the incident, but the Americans took it all in stride, acting calmly and coolly.

☝ MEANWHILE, IN AMERICA...

Countless Americans were being rounded up and interrogated without charges or warrants because someone had named them as being "Communist", whatever that means. Proceedings that would make Robespierre blush were carried out constantly as the U.S. rooted out the dreaded scourge that had infiltrated every sector of society. Senator Joseph "Charlie" McCarthy led the charge, and his efforts to quell the Communist uprising resulted in the persecution of over 10,000 people. These heinous individuals included hard-line Communist spokespeople like Albert Einstein, Charlie Chaplin, and Orson Welles. The cry "Better Dead Than Red" went up across the nation. (Please note that almost all of the adults who cried this out are now dead. I guess they got their wish...)

Seeing as how the Soviet Union owned ½ of Europe, ½ of Asia, ½ of Africa, and ⅖ of the North Pole, the Western World decided to form a union of countries that would defend our collective freedom, as well as Santa Claus. That organization is called NATO, which stands for whatever America wants it to.

With the U.S. taking the lead in the fight against Communism, Canada was free to explore options that would keep the peace

IN TODAY'S NEWS, PEACEKEEPERS WERE DROPPED INTO A HOT ZONE IN BLUGARDNITZE. THEIR GENERAL SAID "WE'LL KEEP THE PEACE, JUST AS SOON AS WE FIND IT!"

without resorting to nuclear explosions. A man who would be our prime minister someday, Lester "Bee" Pearson, developed a novel idea that grew into a permanent U.N. institution: peace keepers. Soldiers are sent from countries around the globe and are then trained and supplied by the United Nations. Their role is to bring peace to trouble spots wherever they pop up, such as Croatia, or Summerside, PEI. Their main strategy for bringing (and keeping) peace is to not shoot their guns. The non-firing guns and blue helmets distract the locals enough that they forget why they're shooting at each other.

A CLASSIC CANADIAN CONVERSATION!

CANADIAN PEACEKEEPER: Excuse me, gentlemen.

TEAM A: Vat do you vant?

TEAM B: Yah, vee are tryink to kill each udder here over long-forgot insult mit basket uv beets.

CANADIAN PEACEKEEPER: Yes, well, the United Nations has decided you should stop.

TEAM A: Vell, if vee stop shooting at each udder, who are vee to shoot?

TEAM B: Perhaps vee should shoot da U.N. guys.

CANADIAN PEACEKEEPER: No, that's not acceptable. If you do, we'll have to point our empty guns at you in a semi-serious manner, eh?

TEAM A: I am liking zat idea, Team B. Und zee blue helmets makes zem easy to see.

PEACEKEEPER: (sigh) Okay, we'll leave.

TEAM A: Goot-bye.

TEAM B: Now, vat vas I doink?

PEACEKEEPER: You were shooting at each other over a stupid feud.

TEAM A: Ah, yes! Zee beets! BANG! BANG!

Canada continues to send peacekeepers all over the world, and they serve our country proudly by not killing anyone. If a UN peacekeeper actually fires a gun, that soldier is deemed "too violent" and is sent to a remote place known to have a violent past, such as Gimli, Manitoba.*

Now, please don't misunderstand me. I have the utmost respect for anyone who dons a uniform and heads to one of the world's hot spots in the hopes of bringing peace. My concern comes when these soldiers getting shot at can't simply defend themselves. Maybe a better/safer tactic would be to bring in extremely loud sound systems that play Question Period re-runs from the 1970's. Less shooting, more snoring.

STUDY QUESTIONS

1. DO YOU REMEMBER YOUR FIRST DATE?
2. IT'S HARD TO BELIEVE THAT CHARLIE CHAPLIN WAS A COMMUNIST, EH?
3. HAVE YOU BEEN TO GIMLI, MANITOBA? DID YOU SEE ANY VIKINGS?

*Settled by Vikings. See Chapter Two.

CHAPTER TWENTY-THREE
THIS BEAT GOES ON, EH?

As the Cold War continued, life in Canada began to change, and not necessarily for the better. Now that the Soviet Union had "the bomb", Canada became the filling in the U.S./U.S.S.R. Nuclear Oreo cookie. Shots fired by either side would pass right over our territory, and that was simply NOT acceptable! But what could be done? The two cookie parts carried on as though the creamy centre was of no concern, which was a grave mistake that would make both powers rue the day they ignored Canadian interests!

Okay, so Canada had given up on being a major military power, and we had shrunk our once-proud navy and air force to an embarrassing level. We could still effectively maintain a military presence over eight square blocks of Ottawa, (and parts of Montréal during the playoffs) so there really wasn't a problem, right? And, after getting rid of our old equipment, we bought even older, second-rate equipment from the Yanks, so the government could feel better about running up the national debt.

To make matters worse, a war popped up in Vietnam. (If you don't know where that is, it's near the equator.) For some crazy reason, the Vietnamese people didn't want foreigners taking all of their natural resources, so they started shooting up the place. Since

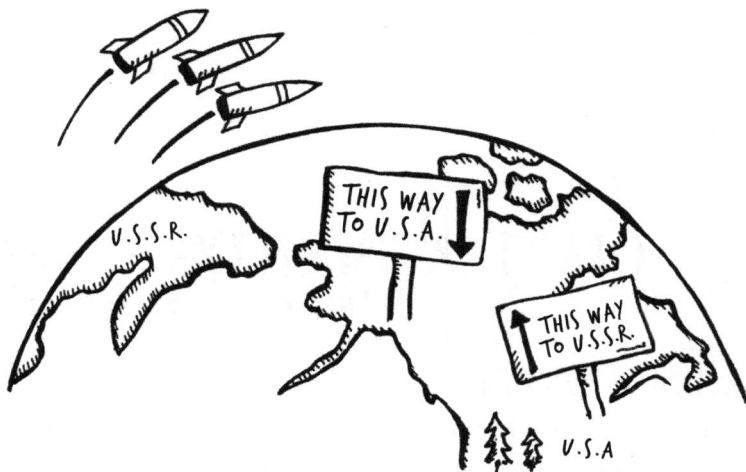

CANADA'S COLD WAR CONTRIBUTION

it had been a French colony, they shot at the French first, until the French got tired of it and the French went home.*

America, wanting to show their allies how to fight a war properly, promptly sent a bunch of 18 year-olds off to the jungles of Southeast Asia. These young men soon found out that the mean streets of New York and Chicago were pretty tame compared with the mean trails of Vietnam. Sure, you could get shot at anywhere, but the mosquitoes, leeches, and snakes were a bit more aggressive there than in Manhattan. Throw in malaria and it was more like Miami in June.

The U.S. quickly set about losing the war. Although there are no doubt many reasons/excuses for the loss, this historian blames Canada. You see, when America went to "save" the Vietnamese people from the evils of Communism by shooting them, a large number of Americans were opposed to the war from

*To France

the start. Many men decided to ignore their government's order to report to the nearest military base for head shaving and push-up practice, and instead ran to Canada. A normal person would call these guys "smart", but running away from military service is sort of frowned upon in the U.S., and these guys were labelled as "draft dodgers". These "dodgers" roamed around Canada passing out flowers and tofu sandwiches until the war was over, at which time they moved back home and formed a professional baseball team.

Why did these guys hide in Canada? Mainly because we didn't have a draft, except beer, and more importantly, Canada didn't make a habit of shooting people on their own soil. These dodgers didn't know a lot about Canada, but they knew what peace looked like. Yes, Canada was gaining a reputation as a peaceful nation, and that was something that U.S. President Lyndon Byron Johnson couldn't stand. LBJ succeeded JFK, who succeeded DDE, but was shot by LHO, and he (LBJ) was trying to get Canada to join him in the Vietnam War. Lester B. Pearson was our Prime Minister at the time and was accosted by LBJ for not joining them in Vietnam. LBP told LBJ that Canadian troops weren't really keen on the high temperatures and humidity of Southeast Asia, but if the Americans invaded Norway, we'd reconsider. LBJ grabbed LBP by the shirt and screamed some nasty acronym-based vulgarities at him. LBP got out while the VP tried to calm LBJ who nevertheless decided to nuke Fargo, North Dakota, not realizing that it was still part of the U.S. Fortunately, he forgot to push the button as he was distracted by the upcoming election, which he lost. Fortunately.

As the Americans were busy losing the Vietnam War, Canada

decided to have its own crisis. In 1963, an extremist group in Québec called the FLQ* was demanding that Québec become a "distinct" society, and demanded that all cereal boxes have French on them. But that was just the start! These folks actually put actual bombs in actual mailboxes trying to kill actual people! In Canada! This went on for years, and in 1970, an event occurred that shook Canada to its core and shaped how our country would look for years to come: I was born. (On another note, that same day** the FLQ kidnapped a British guy who was actually on their side.) To ensure the safety of my family and that of my future wife, (born six days earlier), Prime Minister Trudeau declared martial law across the country! This is the only time this has happened in the one hundred-something years of our country's existence, so, you're welcome.

"CONGRATULATIONS, MRS. PURDY! TRUDEAU JUST DECLARED MARTIAL LAW! ... OH AND IT'S A BOY!"

The FLQ was pretty much wiped out in Canada thanks to the government buying them all one-way flights to Cuba. It may seem like an easy way out after all the terror and such, but you must remember that Cuba is really hot, and it gets hit by hurricanes every couple of years. Also, they still had Castro at this time, and he wasn't very pleasant to North Americans, even if they spoke French with a funny accent.

*According to Google, this means "Front de Libération du Québec". This is obviously wrong as this that would be "FDLDQ".
**My birthday

All of this unpleasantness was forgotten a couple of years later when an extremely pivotal event happened, and I'm not talking about my second birthday. An incredibly talented hockey team consisting of NHL stars was put together for a friendly eight-game series against the Soviets.

Our generous Canadian spirit showed the world that we wanted to share our hockey expertise with not-so-good hockey countries, like the Soviet Union and Angola. In fact, our spirit was so generous that we only won one game in the first five, although we did tie one, too. Then, to the delight of Canadian hockey fans everywhere, we decided to show our actual hockey spirit by trying to kill the German referee.

But, like any good Hollywood movie*, things turned out okay in the end. We won the final three games of the series to reclaim our standing as the Greatest Hockey Country in the History of the Universe, and those immortal words spoken by Foster Hewitt still ring through Canadians' minds today: "Conscription if necessary, but not Paul Henderson!" The Soviets disputed our 'victory' in their newspaper, saying that although they got second at this hockey series, Canada got second to last. (It's like these guys were writing scripts for the B.C. Liberals forty years too soon.)

Canada remained fairly calm for the next few years, but any country that is next to the United States always looks like it's taking a collective nap, especially during the wind up of the Vietnam War, something Americans love to discuss over fondue. Try it. Anyways, Canadians were wanting a bit more excitement and the Québécois were willing to provide it.

The 1976 Olympic Games came to Canada, specifically to Montréal, and the people were very happy to have the world come

*Yes, there have been a couple

to their fair city, congested though it was. Mayor Jean "Curtains" Drapeau was so confident of the success of the Games that when some people warned him of the expenses, he scoffed that "a host city could no more lose money on the Olympics than a man can have a baby!" Proving that he was indeed not a prophet, Montréal proceeded to lose a bajillion dollars on the Games. They didn't even finish building the main stadium until twenty years later, at which time it collapsed.

Given that the city took a bath on the Olympics, people suggested that Mayor Drapeau have a water birth.

STUDY QUESTIONS

1. WHAT IS YOUR FAVOURITE PART OF THE OREO COOKIE?

2. CAN YOU NAME A GOOD HOLLYWOOD MOVIE BESIDES STAR WARS? (YES, EPISODE IV)

3. CAN YOU BELIEVE IT TOOK US 23 CHAPTERS TO TAKE A SHOT AT THE B.C. LIBERALS? NEITHER CAN WE.

CHAPTER TWENTY-FOUR
THE AWESOME 80'S, EH!

The 1980's began with a shock: the U.S. national hockey team won a game. Now the stuff of legends, a day doesn't go by without some reference to the defeat of the Evil Communist Soviet Red Army hockey club at the Lake Placid Winter Olympics. Movies, books, songs, and dances all celebrate that historic event.

A few months later, the Summer Olympics were held in Moscow. Sensing that the Soviets were seeking some drastic measure of revenge, the U.S. boycotted the games, and 'suggested' that the rest of the free world do the same. They gave some crazy reason for the boycott like the Soviet invasion of Afghanistan, but we know better. The Western boycott allowed the Soviet Union to sweep the medals in every event, except for one gold in women's swimming, which was won by an East German man.

As these monumental events mercilessly unfolded around the world, Canadians set about de-selecting/selecting/de-selecting/re-selecting a prime minister. Pierre Trudeau had apparently run out of "street-cred" and was replaced by Joe "Who?" Clark, whose theme song was from the great Canadian band, Trooper, and said, "here for a good time, not a long time." Unfortunately for Clark, the time was neither "good" nor "long" and before you could say "non-confidence vote", Trudeau was back on the throne.

It was obvious, though, that Pierre's days were numbered, but he wasn't about to go quietly. Within the last few years of his reign, he ran up the national debt from $1.46 to over $170 billion. "Gotta spend money to make money!" he shouted from his new yacht.

One notable thing Trudeau did accomplish in his waning years was to repatriate the constitution. We aren't entirely sure what this means, but this historian was actually at the repatriation ceremony in Ottawa, although he was too short to see anything. The gist is, we think, that Canada could now take full responsibility for itself. We could do all sorts of things that we couldn't before, and our parents (Britain) were freed from being held responsible for our screw-ups. It was like a national bar mitzvah, but without the Manischewitz.

Speaking of screw-ups, John Turner became prime minister soon after, as Trudeau quietly retired from politics. As the story goes, Trudeau went for a walk in the snow, looking for a sign that he should stay in power. After getting his tongue stuck to a lamp post, he decided to focus on more important things, namely, not losing the next election.

Speaking of screw-ups, Brian Mulroney won the next election and uttered a phrase that still makes this historian shudder: "Give us twenty years and you won't recognize this country." *Shudder*.

There are things one must realize about Mulroney, and I will share them with you. One, he's short. He's, like, five feet tall. He always appeared tall on television, but that's because he wouldn't come down off the steps until the last camera van had turned the corner. He'd also sit during most interviews, usually on a Greater Toronto phone book, with Yellow Pages.

MULRONEY'S FIRST SPEECH ON T.V.

Two, he lied.* Before the 1984 federal election, he droned on and on about how evil Free Trade would be and how it would destroy Canada to get into "economic bed" with the U.S. Ten minutes after gaining power, he not only crawled into bed with the U.S., he ordered room service and charged it to Canadians. Here is a sample of Brian's "to-do" list during his reign:

Step One: Bring in Free Trade with the United States.

Step Two: Force the sale of gobs of Canadian businesses to rich Americans.

Step Three: Get Canadians to buy goods formerly made here, but now made in New Jersey.

Step Four: Notice that your government is losing billions in revenue that used to come from duty and taxes placed on American goods.

Step Five: Bring in the Goods and Services Tax so you can recoup the lost revenue from your own people, since you don't want to upset the Americans.

*Well, duh.

Step Six: Distract everyone from what's going on by speaking in a really deep voice and running up the national debt to over ½ a trillion dollars.

Step Seven: Watch *Knight Rider*.

After this process had completed itself, Brian Mulroney's popularity had plummeted to the lowest level of any Canadian prime minister in history, but hovered slightly above most STDs. It stood at *minus* 14%, and, if the story can be believed, even he woke up one morning and said, "I'm an idiot", but it was too late and Canada was both broke and had a nasty social itch.

♛MEANWHILE, IN AMERICA...

The Americans were so happy with Free Trade, and how it strengthened their own economy, that they invited Mexico to join, then moved all their business there, which weakened their own economy.

Here's a fun fact: *over half* of Canada's debt, from 1867 to now, was incurred by Mulroney in nine years.

I guess he didn't need twenty years after all.

STUDY QUESTIONS

1. DID YOU EVER SEE PICTURES OF THE EAST GERMAN WOMEN'S SWIM TEAM?
2. DID YOU NOTICE THAT WE NEVER DESCRIBED JOHN TURNER'S REIGN? *(YOU'RE WELCOME)*
3. DID YOU SEE THE KNIGHT RIDER EPISODE WHERE KITT RAN OVER MULRONEY?
   OR WAS THAT JUST SOME MAGICAL DREAM?

CHAPTER TWENTY-FIVE
THE LIBERALS SAVE US ALL!

The next decade opened for Canada with the Edmonton Oilers winning their fifth Stanley Cup, Brian Mulroney cancelling Federal Family Allowance payments, and Molly Dunsworth being born.* Yes, it promised to be an exciting decade, and thanks to the abolition of leaded gasoline the environmental damage to the planet would be reversed and our children would inherit a clean world, devoid of any polluted air, lakes, forests, slums, etc. Utopia, here we come!

Fast-forward to 1991 and we discovered: the ozone layer had holes in it, second hand-smoke is bad for you, drinking while driving and/or pregnant may cause problems, and all the damage done by leaded gasoline was the least of our worries. But there was hope! All that we humans had to do was stop driving, stop eating meat, stop watering our lawns, and buy recycled toilet paper, which sounds a lot worse now that I actually wrote it down. If we did these things, the Earth would heal herself and become that paradise we all want for the future!

This message of hope was brought to us by Greenpeace, which began in Vancouver in 1970. From this pristine location of a bajillion cars gridlocked on whichever street you are travelling

---

*She played opposite Rutger Hauer in Hobo With a Shotgun. No, we haven't seen it, either.

down, Greenpeace preached its message from the rooftops, street corners, and their ancient, leaky, diesel-guzzling boat called "The Rainbow Warrior". A spokesperson admitted that the ship wasn't exactly up to the environmental standards they demanded of everyone else, but with your donations, they could buy another one just like it.

The 90's also saw the federal Conservatives' power wane, and in 1993, sensing a disaster, Mulroney retired from politics. There was no magical walk in the snow for Brian, and no crystal ball was required to know that the end was nigh. He simply grabbed his vast wealth and toddled off to parts unknown, leaving the disaster in Kim Campbell's hands. Using a strategy rarely seen in Canadian politics, Campbell (former Minister of Defense) chose to threaten the Canadian voter by saying, "Don't mess with me, I've got tanks." Unfortunately for her, due to budget cutbacks, the tanks had no guns on them, and were currently being used to deliver FTD flower bouquets to senators' mistresses.

The 1993 federal election was a landmark event for a few reasons. The ruling party before the election wasn't even an official party *after* the election. The "Progressive" Conservatives went from a majority of 169 seats all the way down to two. Another reason that this election was an important moment is that the Bloc Québécois became the Official Opposition. Yep, a federal party that only runs in one province was now speaking for everyone who didn't vote for the federal Liberals. To put names to this weirdness, Québec separatists were now the voice of Alberta in Ottawa. Only in Canada, eh?

Under Jean Chrétien, the Liberals did pretty well, and the national debt actually went *down* about $100 billion, which sounds like a lot unless you're talking about Canada's national debt, which we are. Chrétien and his Finance Minister Paul "Show Me the Money" Martin would travel around the globe telling all the stupid countries how to balance their grossly mismanaged chequebooks. Financial leaders would sit with rapt attention as these two geniuses spelled out, at great length, how they saved the Canadian economy: "We never returned Clinton's calls, eh?" The rest of the world rushed out to do the same, but by then George Bush Jr. was in, and they already knew to ignore him.

As the 1990's closed, Canadians joined the rest of the globe in a collective brace awaiting the impact of the dreaded Y2K, the greatest calamity to befall humankind since the NBA brought a team to Vancouver. According to top-notch scientists and conspiracy nuts alike, the computers that ran every aspect of our lives would not comprehend what to do when their internal clocks reached January 1st, 2000. When this moment hit, billions of people would be plunged into darkness and chaos! Defying all laws of physics, planes, kites, and even birds would fall out of the sky, cars would drive into the nearest river, and microwaves would stop in the middle of preparing the bag of popcorn, leaving nothing but hot kernels, much like they usually did.

Canada was fortunate to be in the perfect geographical location to watch the global madness unfold. Thanks to the invention of time zones,* Canada would be one of the last countries to be affected by the dreaded technological apocalypse, with Newfoundland being hit a half hour later. The first country to experience the chaos would be New Zealand, and the indigenous peoples, called Hobbits, prepared for the worst.

*See "Neato Almost-Canadians"

10 SECONDS BEFORE Y2K   10 SECONDS AFTER Y2K

"HEY! THE LEAFS ARE STILL   "WELL, MAYBE NEXT YEAR"
IN THE PLAYOFF HUNT!"

As midnight on New Year's Eve came and went without a problem, most of the world relaxed, realizing that the dire warnings had all been for naught. They returned to their late night movies and burnt popcorn kernels, and all the flying objects, planes and birds alike, landed safely. It was a rather anti-climactic conclusion to a much-anticipated event, just like the Super Bowl half-time show.

But back to Canada and the glorious situation we found ourselves in at the hands of the Liberals. Gone were the days of the Mulroney government's habit of throwing Canadian money at the Americans. Now we enjoyed the Chrétien government's tight-fisted, Grinch-like budgets that not only saved them billions of dollars, but also shut down schools and clinics at an alarming rate. Police, fire, ambulance? Cut back! To paraphrase Paul Martin: "Why are we paying for these services 24/7? I mean, it's not like there's a fire every day, eh?" Soon, the government was awash in money and Canadians were enjoying extended stays in hotels while their burned-out homes were looted. And, thanks to the cut backs in nursing care, Grandma would come and live at the hotel, too! (All part of the Liberal's promise to "keep families together!")

Thankfully, Canadians soon got wise to this sort of monetary shenanigans, and Chrétien retired under intense pressure from a former friend, Paul Martin. You know the guy who travelled the world to share in the glory of Chrétien's fiscal policies? Yeah, that guy. Well, he turned on his boss and forced him out of office. Faster than you could say "rising deficit", Canada was safely in the warm and familiar embrace of crushing debt, and our dollar plummeted to 70 cents U.S.

Ah, there's no place like home!

STUDY QUESTIONS

1. HAVE YOU EVER DRIVEN IN VANCOUVER? DID YOU FIND PARKING? EXPLAIN.
2. ISN'T MICROWAVE POPCORN TERRIBLE?
3. WHO WOULD YOU LIKE TO SEE IN THE SUPER BOWL HALFTIME SHOW?

CHAPTER TWENTY-SIX
THE NEW MILLENNIUM IS HERE!

In 2000, Canada was still under the guidance of Chrétien and the Liberals, and they were constantly moving us away from a dependence on American trade. Trying to open doors in Asia, Chrétien rode a bicycle in China, sold some Candu nuclear reactors in India, and ate shark-fin soup in Japan. When he realized that this last act was frowned upon back home, he simply said, "I didn't swallow."

2001 will always be remembered for the terrible acts of terrorism in the U.S., and Canadians lent a helping hand in many ways during that time. The people of Gander, Newfoundland have received worldwide acclaim for their role in making many diverted passengers feel at home, despite the fact none of the guests could understand them. (See Chapter Twenty-One)

☗MEANWHILE, IN AMERICA...

Americans were duly enraged at the attacks, and the people demanded action. When the information surfaced that the majority of attackers came from Saudi Arabia, and that the money to support the attackers came from Saudi Arabia, the American military machine quickly leapt into action and invaded Iraq.

1966

So, CANADA, Y'ALL GONNA JOIN US IN KILLIN' REDS IN VIETNAM?

No, BUT THANKS FOR ASKING, EH?

PREZ

P.M.

2001

So, CANADA, Y'ALL GONNA JOIN US IN KILLIN' ARABS IN IRAQ?

No, BUT THANKS FOR ASKING, EH?

PREZ

P.M.

As supportive as we were of the stranded passengers, we simply couldn't accept the invitation from President George "Double-U" Bush to join them in bombing Iraq into the Stone Age. Although the number of American allies in the invasion was impressive,* Canada politely declined to join their ranks. This sent Canadian/ American relations spiralling down to a level not seen since we told them we weren't going to shoot Vietnamese people just to stop the Russians. As it turns out, the U.S.'s intelligence community's reports had more errors than a late-season Blue Jays' game, and there was an obvious lack of "weapons of mass destruction".

*One

Canada came out of that crisis looking pretty smart, while the Americans re-elected George. It's like the Universe couldn't make up its mind.

We did help to free Afghanistan from the evil clutches of the Taliban. Our non-peacekeeping soldiers once again showed the world why we're more than tree-hugging, moose-eating, plaid-wearing, ice-fishing, beer-drinking curlers. Sure, we are all those things to a degree, but we also fight for others when they need it, even if they have no oil.

Canadians can be quick to point out other countries' mistakes, but that's just because our own government is awash with them. We know that watching one sitting of the House of Commons is like seeing hundreds of bobble-heads bouncing around while whomever is in power just spends our hard-earned tax money on foolish things, while we can't find affordable daycare. When we ask them to please look out for the average Canadian, the bobble-heads look around the room they all sit in, figure that all Canadians make $120,000 a year and get free lunches and plane tickets and hotels rooms, and wonder, "so what's the problem?"

Okay, that's not totally fair. Not *all* the bobble-heads think that. Some actually care about their constituents enough to have one of their secretaries send out a form letter to let you know that they received your note asking to raise child support a few bucks to match inflation. The letter will read something like this:

Dear Occupant,

This letter is let you know that I received your letter. Thank you for your letter. I have read your letter. It was a good letter, with many letters making many words. You certainly write well for a poor person. Anyways, I have read your request and I feel confident that, with enough time and resources, I can prepare an ad-hoc committee that will research how to respond to your request in a succinct and professional manner. This is what we call "tax dollars in action!"

Sincerely,

Larry "Spud" Hogwash.
P.S. Vote for me, eh?

As you can clearly see, there was no way we were ever going to invade Iraq.

STUDY QUESTIONS

1. WHY DO THE BLUE JAYS ALWAYS LOSE IN AUGUST?
2. DO YOU HAVE A BOBBLE-HEAD? IS IT OF A TORONTO BLUE JAY?
3. DID YOU VOTE FOR LARRY? SO, IT'S YOUR FAULT, EH?

CHAPTER TWENTY-SEVEN
AND HERE WE ARE...

Two years after Paul Martin became the prime minister, he wisely called an election. I don't say "wisely" because he lost to the Conservatives under Stephen "Let it Ride" Harper. It was wise of Martin because if he didn't call an election at that time, there was a really good chance that his own party would have used him for a piñata at the annual Liberal Party Siesta Fiesta, which is still going on today.

Under Harper's watchful gaze since 2006, Canada has been an active participant in global events such as: trade agreements with China, sporting events with China, military training exercises with China, and environmental agreements with the Devil, who was sitting in for China. The last point has been an agreement to continue to belch out lots of pollution in order to keep people employed* so they can feed their families and we can buy all sorts of neato consumer gadgets like lead-covered baby cribs.

Speaking of the environment, the Alberta Oil Sands have come under scrutiny recently, and many countries and environmental groups have demanded a reduction in the output of this heinous product that fuels the busses the protestors have ridden to get to the Oil Sands. Harper, always wanting to listen and respond to

*Chinese people

Canadians' concerns, promptly sold the Oil Sands to environmentally-conscientious countries, such as China. "Now it's their problem," he said while on a trade mission to Saudi Arabia to find cheap oil.

Harper enjoyed a majority government, and passed laws left and right in a flurry of activity, hoping to leave his mark on Canada in the same way Mulroney did. Many of the bills were passed in the "omnibus" fashion, which basically means that a bajillion laws were crammed into one reading, which certainly saved time.

SANTA'S NAUGHTY   A TYPICAL CONSERVATIVE
OR NICE LIST   OMNIBUS BILL

During the Harper administration, I had predicted the following omnibus bill to be passed: Bill C-177, a bill that would include, among a hundred other laws, the enabling of judges to sentence teachers to a minimum 3-year incarceration for handing out 'zeroes'. Teachers would respond by handing out -1% scores instead. Students would then protest by texting their MP's (during class) but to no avail.

What most Canadians will remember about this time is the lack of trust the public had for government officials. Of course, this isn't new, but the fact that we trust government less than lawyers and bankers should have us worried. It must be noted that similar poll results were found right before Rome fell.

But what could possibly cause this drastic drop in the trust level between the governed and governing? I think a good example would be a $16 glass of orange juice. Our International Co-operation Minister in 2012 was Bev Oda. She was supposed to strengthen Canada's relationship to other countries, and to help those countries develop into stronger economies. Apparently, Bev figured she'd help out the poor citrus-growing nation of Florida. Then, while in London, England, she upgraded from a five-star hotel to Buckingham Palace because "they have better tea." Also, she needed a limousine to get to and fro because "the taxis smell funny." It must be noted that all of this occurred while she was attending a conference on how to help the world's most destitute children. This is just one more example of the irony oft-repeated here in Canada.

There are many more, to be sure, and one only needs to pick up the most recent paper to read about more of our tax dollars being misspent. Canadian governments aren't ignorant (don't quote me on that) and they know that we love to drive, so they crank up taxes on gas, citing the desperate need for road repair, and in return they fix almost 12% of the pot holes on the Trans-Canada highway in Saskatchewan.

Canadians also love to experiment with different governments. Even Alberta, a stronghold of Conservative politics since forever, voted in an NDP majority government just to "see what happens." Going from a long-standing, far-right government to one with policies just a ruble to the left of Lenin, it shouldn't have been too difficult to predict certain changes. The average citizen would have less money in his or her pocket, but his or her child's daycare could now afford story books in both official languages. This made the Albertans very, very happy indeed.

Since this is a history book, and the Alberta election I mentioned above happened yesterday, I will end it here. There very well might be more history that happens in Canada between this writing and your reading, but the most important stuff is certainly contained in these pages. So, feel confident in your knowledge of Canadian history, and how it is rich and vibrant. Tell your friends to seek out more information about our heritage as a nation. Tell your friends that Canadian history is just as important to the current state of the world as, say, Guatemala's. But most of all, tell your friends to buy this book.

SYMBOLS OF ALBERTA

BEFORE 2015   AFTER 2015

STUDY QUESTION

IN CELEBRATION OF YOUR SUCCESSFUL COMPLETION OF THIS BOOK, WE'RE GIVING YOU A BREAK ON THE STUDY QUESTIONS. IF YOU ARE THE TYPE OF PERSON WHO READS THE LAST PAGE FIRST, WE'RE NOT GIVING ANY PLOT LINES AWAY HERE. IF THAT DISAPPOINTS YOU, WE'RE SORRY, EH?

CHAPTER TWENTY-EIGHT
A BONUS CHAPTER AT NO EXTRA COST!

Well, lucky you. I decided to write this book during a federal election year, although I had no idea it would happen because the government never told me first. Jerks.

Anyways, the election took place and Steven "Balanced Budget at Any Cost" Harper was defeated by Justin "What's a budget?" Trudeau. Canadians turned out in near-record numbers to vote, which is always encouraging, and thanks to the "First Past the Post" election system we have in Canada, our current leader won a majority of seats in the House of Commons with a whopping 26% of registered voters' support. But he didn't take long to make sweeping changes to the Canadian political and social landscape. Shortly after the election, he was overheard saying, "Sure, I'm going to run up the national debt, but I'm legalizing pot, so people will be too stoned to care."

Although Harper and Trudeau stole most of the show during the lead up to election day, there were many others who jostled for the votes of Canadians. These people ran very effective campaigns, using passionate speeches, colourful advertising, and clever spin-doctoring to get people on board with their viewpoints. These people stayed up until the wee hours of the night, seven days a week, fairly chaining themselves to their workstations until their bodies collapsed in a heap. These people were, of course, my "friends" on Facebook.

In this age of instant global communication, it is painfully obvious that everyone will have an opinion that must be shared with all humans *right now* or else we risk an alien invasion, a zombie apocalypse, or something much worse, like health care cuts. Regardless of your political bent, you could be absolutely confident that someone, usually someone you had never even met, would eloquently and passionately discuss with you any given political issue, and that this discussion would ultimately culminate in that person calling you a "poo-poo head". This is unfortunate, especially in Canada, as we have a global image of "nice-ness" we have to uphold, with the 2011 Vancouver riot being a minor blip. But back to the aftermath of the election.

I was fortunate, in that my friends ranged from the "Far Right" to the "We Love Mao" camps, and I almost cancelled my satellite subscription as *nothing* was as amusing as the back-and-forth that scrolled up and down my computer screen. People who knew pretty much zero about how government is elected or administered were telling everyone how to do it. It was like listening to Question Period. Unfortunately, that conversation hasn't slowed down much since the election.

Pundits on both sides continue to smear the candidates as though the election is still happening. People blame Harper for *causing*: global warming, the national debt, the Blue Jays' early playoff exit, and that Justin Bieber has more tattoos than the average federal inmate. Meanwhile, Trudeau is being blamed for *not fixing*: global warming, the national debt, the Blue Jays' early playoff exit, and the FLQ crisis (see Chapter Twenty-Three), the last one being lamented by pot-smokers who think it's still 1970 and are wondering how Pierre suddenly got such nice hair. To be honest, we really have nothing serious to complain about here in the Great White North. We truly enjoy a wonderful existence here, can laugh at our mistakes, and we don't take ourselves too seriously. This is in stark contrast to Germany, which was recently voted as the "least humourous country on planet Earth". When the German people were told of this finding, they tried to disprove it by invading Belgium, which has always been the "go-to" answer for uptight Germans. Alas, this all happened during *Octoberfest*, and by the time that was done, they had forgotten the global slight and went back to making high-performance automobiles. Watching hairy men in lederhosen play the accordion will make you forget pretty much anything. The strong beer is just a bonus.

As Canada moves forward in this century, there will be many exciting moments that will continue to shape the country's reputation, the citizens, and even the landscape. These moments will be as ground-breaking as Women's Suffrage (Chapter Nineteen), the Battle of the Plains of Abraham (Chapter Six), or, if I may, Confederation (Chapter Eleven)! I suspect that some future historian will make observations about these moments, scrawl them down, and then sell them to some unsuspecting publishing house.

BONUS CHAPTER STUDY QUESTIONS

1. DID YOU VOTE IN THE 2015 CANADIAN FEDERAL ELECTION? DID FACEBOOK HELP?

2. DO YOU LOVE MAO?

3. HAVE YOU EVER WORN LEDERHOSEN? EXPLAIN.

NEATO ALMOST-CANADIANS!

In this section of the book, we are going to introduce you to some Canadians who have made quite the impact on our fair land, despite the fact that they weren't even born here, and, if they were born "here", well, Canada wasn't even a country yet. Obviously, this list could go on for many, many pages, (and I just thought of another book I could write) so we have tried to keep the list to those names most Canadians will recognize. If you don't, do not feel badly. Learn all you can and then go watch curling. (Note: we only put their birth dates down, as we wanted to keep this a happy book!)

INVENTORS AND INNOVATORS

Alexander Graham Bell
(1847 – Edinburgh, Scotland)
Made the first telephone, but had no one to call.

Tommy Douglas
(1904 – Falkirk, Scotland)
Douglas brought about Universal Health Care, but you have to be sick to use it.

Sir John A. Macdonald
(1815 – Glasgow, Scotland)
Macdonald invented Canada, mainly to tick off the U.S. (See Chapter Eleven)

Sir Sanford Fleming
(1827 – Kirkcaldy, UK)
He invented Time Zones, and by extension, Jet Lag. Thanks a lot, eh.

Jean Vanier
(1928 – Geneva, Switzerland)
The founder of L'Arche, proving that people with mental challenges are a vital and vibrant part of our community.

MILITARY LEADERS
Sir Isaac Brock
(1769 – St. Peter Port, UK)
Brock bravely led British forces in the defense of Upper Canada during the War of 1812, scoring many notable victories over superior American forces. (See Chapter Eight)

James Wolfe
(1727 – Westerham, UK)
Wolfe ordered a daring British attack on Québec City that led to the defeat of the French in North America. (See Chapter Six)

Joseph Brant
(1743 – Somewhere in the northern U.S.)
He was a native leader who fought on the British side during the American Revolution.

Romeo Dallaire
(1946 – Denekamp, Netherlands)
Dallaire was the UN Peacekeeping General in Rwanda during the genocide, and is now a world-famous champion of human rights.

Sam Steele
(1848 – Bracebridge, United Province of Canada)
Steele kept the peace in the Klondike during the Gold Rush in 1898. (See Chapter Sixteen)

Tecumseh
(1768 – Scioto River, Ohio)
He was a Shawnee leader and an ally to the British and Canadians in the War of 1812.

EXPLORERS
Simon Fraser
(1776 – New York when it was a British colony)
Fraser mapped a large portion of British Columbia and invented a river.

Alexander MacKenzie
(1764 – Stornoway, UK)
Mapped a large portion of the northwest of Canada and invented a river, just like Fraser. (See above)

ATHLETES
Steve Nash
(1974 – Johannesburg, South Africa)
Nash was an NBA star who won the Most Valuable Player two years in a row.

Louis Cyr
(1863 – Saint-Cyprien-de-Napierville, Québec)
The strongest man to have ever lived. He ate what four men would each meal, and sometimes their food, too. Then he'd carry them home.

ENTREPRENEURS AND BUILDERS
William Van Horne
(1843 – Frankfort, Illinois)
He was the President of the Canadian Pacific Railway. (A Canadian business owned by an American? Don't act so surprised.)

Lt. Col. John By
(1779 – London, England)
He oversaw the building of the Rideau Canal that has 50 dams and 47 locks and connects Ottawa and Kingston. (The canal is located near this historian's childhood home.)

NEATO ACTUAL-CANADIANS!

And here are a few Canucks who were actually born here, and did quite well as simple Canadians just trying to make their world a better place. Of course, some of them did so well that they had to move to the U.S. to spread all things Canadian. (And get paid in American dollars.) Again, this list could go on for many, many volumes, but we believe this is a good sampling of the indomitable Canadian spirit!

INVENTORS AND INNOVATORS
The Famous Five:
Nellie McClung, Emily Murphy,
Irene Parlby, Louise McKinney,
and Henrietta Edwards
(obviously a variety of birthdates)
They spearheaded the "Persons Case" which laid the groundwork for changing how women are treated before the law in Canada. Due to their efforts, women can now vote, purchase and own property, and hold political office.

Bill Gibson
(1876 – Balgonie, Saskatchewan)
Also known as the "Balgonie Birdman", his was the first Canadian-built airplane, which flew over 200 feet on the first flight in 1909.

David Suzuki
(1936 – Vancouver, BC)
Suzuki is an environmental activist and scientist who has made Canadians aware of the interconnectedness of life, and how we're screwing it all up.

Sir Frederick Banting
(1891 – Alliston, Ontario)
He was the Nobel laureate (not sure what that means) who first developed and used insulin on humans. Diabetics live better and longer thanks to his efforts.

Marc Garneau
(1949 – Québec City)
He was the first Canadian in space, if you don't include William Shatner and James Doohan in Star Trek.

Roberta Bondar
(1945 – Sault Ste. Marie, Ontario)
She was the first Canadian female astronaut, as well as the first neurologist in space.

MILITARY MEN
Billy Bishop
(1894 – Owen Sound, Ontario)
He was the top Canadian WWI ace who shot down a bajillion enemy planes.

Roy Brown
(1893 – Carleton Place, Ontario)
Brown is officially credited with shooting down the Red Baron, Germany's dreaded ace fighter pilot.

Tommy Prince
(1915 – Scanterbury, Manitoba)
Prince was the most decorated First Nations soldier of World War II and the Korean War. He won twelve medals, mainly for bravery, and served with the joint Canadian/American special force known as "The Devil's Brigade".

ENTERTAINERS

Michael J. Fox
(1961 – Edmonton, Alberta)
He is a star of films and TV, and founded the Michael J. Fox Foundation for Parkinson's research.

Doug Henning
(1947 – Winnipeg, Manitoba)
Henning was a great magician who made things disappear. The government tried to hire him to be Finance Minister to make national debt disappear, but he said he only did "magic", not "miracles".

Céline Dion
(1968 – Charlemagne, Québec)
Dion is one of the most successful singers in history, in both official languages.

Megan Follows
(1968 – Toronto, Ontario)
Actress who provided millions with an unforgettable look at Anne (of Green Gables) Shirley.

Lorne Greene
(1915 – Ottawa, Ontario)
Actor who worked in outer space, the Wild West, and in Lorne Greene's New Wilderness.

John Candy
(1950 – Newmarket, Ontario)
He was a star of many films, as well as Canada's own SCTV comedy show.

Jim Carrey
(1962 – Newmarket, Ontario)
Born in the same town as John Candy, Carrey is a Hollywood star of film and TV, and he will find your missing pet.

Don Cherry
(1934 – Kingston, Ontario)
Cherry is a patriotic Canadian hockey analyst who wears the wackiest suits and supports our troops.

Alex Trebek
(1940 – Sudbury, Ontario)
A fully-bilingual man, Trebek is known best for hosting Jeopardy! Famous Canadians for $500? *Answer:* He has the record for being the longest-running TV game show host.

Anne Murray
(1945 – Springhill, Nova Scotia)
One of the most successful performers in Canadian history, Anne Murray has sold over 50 million albums worldwide, and gave the term "Snowbird" to describe Canadians who run to Florida at the sight of the first snowflake.

INSPIRING ATHLETES
Wayne Gretzky
(1961 – Brantford, Ontario)
The hockey phenomenon who re-wrote the record books many times over, and whom, in 1988, was the object of arguably the most stunning trade in sports history.

Larry Walker
(1966 – Maple Ridge, BC)
Walker was a baseball star who began with the Montréal Expos (remember them?) and won many awards, including National League MVP.

Terry Fox
(1958 – Winnipeg, Manitoba)
Terry Fox is definitely the most inspirational person this historian knows. Terry suffered from cancer, and, after losing his right leg, he decided to run across Canada to raise money and awareness for cancer research. On average, he ran the equivalent of a marathon every day for 143 straight days, for a total of 5,373 kms.

ENTREPRENEURS
Scott Abbott
(Montreal, Québec) and
Chris Haney
(1950 – Welland, Ontario)
These two were the creators of the widely-successful game
Trivial Pursuit. For a piece of the pie, and the win, when was
Scott Abbott born?

JUST DOWNRIGHT GOOD CANUCKS, EH!
John McCrae
(1872 – Guelph, Ontario)
The author of "In Flanders Fields", he was Canada's WWI
poet soldier. His poignant poem is repeated every year on
Remembrance Day.

Norman Bethune
(1890 – Gravenhurst, Ontario)
Bethune was a doctor who worked to help both soldiers and
civilians in war-torn China. He developed the mobile surgery
hospital, so, in a way, he gave us M*A*S*H.

CPSIA information can be obtained
at www.ICGtesting.com
Printed in the USA
LVHW080502150719
624092LV00010B/188/P